EXTRAORDINARY LEADERS
IN EXTRAORDINARY TIMES

Extraordinary Leaders in Extraordinary Times

UNADORNED CLAY POT MESSENGERS

Volume 1

Edited by

H. Stanley Wood

WILLIAM B. EERDMANS PUBLISHING COMPANY
GRAND RAPIDS, MICHIGAN / CAMBRIDGE, U.K.

Wm. B. Eerdmans Publishing Co.
255 Jefferson Ave. S.E., Grand Rapids, Michigan 49503 /
P.O. Box 163, Cambridge CB3 9PU U.K.

Printed in the United States of America

11 10 09 08 07 06   7 6 5 4 3 2 1

Library of Congress Cataloging-in-Publication Data

Extraordinary leaders in extraordinary times:
unadorned clay pot messengers / edited by H. Stanley Wood
p.   cm.
Includes bibliographical references.
ISBN-10: 0-8028-2977-5 / ISBN-13: 978-0-8028-2977-1 (pbk.: alk. paper)
1. Church development, New.   I. Wood, H. Stanley.
BV652.24.E88   2006
254'.1 — dc22

2006032062

www.eerdmans.com

Contents

Contents

Acknowledgments

A study of this magnitude is often launched with the assurance of major funding and the cooperative partnership of many entities. This research was launched with notification that the Lilly Endowment had funded the study "New Church Development for the 21st Century."

Special thanks must also be given to the Lutheran Brotherhood, which generously funded this study. Of special note is the preparatory work for the study done by Robert S. Hoyt, former leader of the Evangelical Lutheran Church in America's office of New Church Development, who wrote the first draft of the study and who engaged the interest of most of the participating denominations. In addition to the Lutheran Brotherhood, seven mainline denominations and one theological seminary also funded the study. These denominations funded the study in amounts proportional to their size and the scope of their new church developments. In alphabetical order the denominations are: Christian Reformed Church, Episcopal Church, Evangelical Lutheran Church in America, Lutheran Church–Missouri Synod, Presbyterian Church (USA), Reformed Church of America, and the United Church of Christ. The Presbyterian Church (USA) national office of New Church Development (NCD) underwrote the costs to compile and to provide the initial interpretation of the quantitative data. Thanks to Keith Wulff, Director of the PC(USA) research office in Louisville. Additionally, Douglas Oldenburg, former president of Columbia Theological Seminary in Decatur (Atlanta area), offered seminary support by matching the funding of the larger participating denominations. Furthermore, he offered the services of Columbia Seminary's Director of the Center for New Church Development as project director of the study.

As a first step, each denomination began gathering NCD data from its respective new church starts. These denominations quickly discovered that their methodologies for collecting NCD data were divergent and their records on NCD were uneven. One continuing benefit from this project is that standardization of NCD documentation is now in place across these different denominations. Words of appreciation are in order to the research offices, and in denominations without such an office, the special assistants enlisted to organize and gather NCD data and to identify NCD founding pastors. Thanks are also given to them for gathering the quantitative survey data from their denominations' NCD pastors.

I am grateful to a dedicated and skilled writing team which includes Carl S. Dudley, who also was our project evaluator, and to Darrell L. Guder and Robert S. Hoyt. I am indebted to Tim Rogers-Martin for research assistance and to my wife, Dar Sessions Wood, for valuable suggestions in writing and for her constant, gracious support. Collectively, their wisdom and insight have made this study stronger. Any remaining errors in the text are my responsibility.

Finally I want to express my appreciation to Reinder VanTil and William B. Eerdmans Jr. for seeing the publication possibilities in this study and for Eerdmans's commitment to print both the first and second volumes of the study findings. Thanks also to the Eerdmans staff.

On behalf of the writing team, I want to thank all the NCD pastors who participated in this groundbreaking study. I especially want to express appreciation and thanks to the Focus Group NCD pastors who generously gave of their time and shared their experiences of being called to the missional ministry of starting new congregations. I want to echo what we heard from these gifted and effective NCD pastors. They readily acknowledge the presence of God's life-giving Spirit in their ministry. It is our prayer that this work contributes to the discernment and calling of NCD leadership for the extension of Christ's kingdom in the twenty-first century.

San Francisco Theological Seminary   H. STANLEY WOOD, PH.D.
San Anselmo, California

Foreword

My grandfather arrived in Montana from Stavanger, Norway, in the early years of the last century. Accompanied by his twelve children, he rode the newly constructed Great Northern Railroad across the country and got off in a mountain valley where a new town was being built. He was a cement worker, and there was work at hand in laying out the sidewalks. More importantly, he was also a lay preacher, and soon was gathering the loggers and railroad workers and the various misfits those frontier settlements attracted into his living room for Bible studies and prayer meetings. He died before I ever knew him, but on the basis of old conversations with my aunts and uncles, it seems that when Lutheran, Presbyterian, and Methodist missionary pastors arrived sometime later, his anarchic converts were domesticated into "proper" congregations. Grandpa Hoiland was the first new church developer (NCD) in my family.

My mother, Evelyn, was next. In her early forties, she organized and developed a Pentecostal congregation in an outlying village in our valley. My father, a butcher with a thriving meat business (he also knew how to handle a hammer), built the church building, played his saxophone, led the signing, and took care of the finances.

I was the third. In 1962 the Presbytery of Baltimore called me to develop a congregation. The site was a cornfield soon to become a Baltimore suburb. I stayed with Christ Our King Presbyterian for twenty-nine years.

And then my son. Thirty-five years, almost to the day, after I had held my first service of worship in Maryland, Eric gathered a few people together in a community just north of Spokane, Washington, that was later organized by Inland Northwest Presbytery as Colbert Presbyterian Church.

The men and women called to prayer and a new life in Christ in my grandpa's living room were assimilated into a number of congregations. The congregations formed by my mother, myself, and my son are flourishing still. Four generations of New Church Development pastors. Maybe NCD is part of our DNA.

*   *   *

I feel extraordinarily lucky — blessed, I think, is the biblical word for it — to have been called to be a New Church Development pastor by the Presbytery of Baltimore.

I had a pretty good idea of what I was called to do. I was to gather a company of men and women to a place of worship and invite them to become a community of men and women following Jesus. I was clear about the task to which I was assigned, but I soon learned that I didn't know how to do it. I felt like I was standing on a concert stage learning how to play the violin before a bunch of people watching me as I learned (a simile I got from novelist Saul Bellow).

But it turned out to be the perfect place and assignment for me to do graduate work in the pastoral vocation. I learned theology "on the ground." I learned the missional nature of the church outside the traditional bounds of "Christendom." I learned to preach and pray without the conventional supporting cast of a building and an organ, and without an experienced laity and a commonly held tradition to back me up.

I also learned that the church body that called me to the work of new church development had very different ideas of what I should be doing. They expected me to develop a church that "looked like a church." They plied me with programs and advice and goals but never bothered to inquire and find out what I was in fact doing, what I was learning. I worked for years outside the margins of their expectations. Lonely years of being ignored by my colleagues because I wasn't "with the program," the institutionally mandated program. Eventually all that changed for the better, but it took fifteen years.

This book provides material for a radical revision of such expectations, diagnosing the tension between leaders who are responsible for the maintenance of existing churches and those with missional responsibilities among the unchurched or de-churched. Demonstrating that there is no conflict but rather a deep mutuality involved in *maintenance* and *missional* (Darrell Guder's terms).

Being a New Church Development pastor is not for everyone, but for those who are, and for those who so designate and call them, this book is a boon. The extensive research and interpretation wonderfully clarify much of what is involved in recognizing, affirming, and developing the vocations of the men and women God is raising up to lead us as we recover our fundamental identity as a missional church.

EUGENE H. PETERSON
Pastor Emeritus
Christ Our King Presbyterian Church
Bel Air, Maryland
and
Professor Emeritus of Spiritual Theology
Regent College
Vancouver, British Columbia

Note on Research and Abbreviations

Quantitative Research

Quantitative Research comes from the Founding Pastor Church Development Survey, a survey completed by 704 pastors from seven denominations who started churches in the 1980s and 1990s. This survey is comprised of fifty-eight questions and is tabulated into five categories based on the size of the churches in which the 704 surveyed pastors served, as follows:

1. Fewer than 100 members, or fewer than 75 worship attendees
2. 101-170 members, or 76-125 worship attendees
3. 171-304 members, or 126-225 worship attendees
4. 305-540 members, or 226-400 worship attendees
5. 541 or more members, or 401 or more worship attendees

In the text that follows, questions from this survey will be referred to as Survey Q-1, Survey Q-2, etc.

Qualitative Research

Qualitative Research is comprised of six focus groups of new-church development pastors who were deemed "effective" or "extraordinary" based on parameters established in this volume. Five of these focus groups involved male pastors who were grouped by the years in which they entered their seventh year with a new church development. A sixth group involved women developers who reached their seventh year between 1987 and 2002. Transcripts of these focus groups will be referred to as follows:

FG 87-89
FG 90-93
FG 94-96
FG 97-00
FG 01-02
FG 87-02

Introduction

My telephone rang yesterday with a call from an executive I know in the Presbyterian Church. In his geographical area, the middle governing body of the denomination is interested in starting a new church. He knows that the kind of leader he will need is unusual; and he knows that, if he wishes the new church to reach its full potential, he cannot call a traditional pastor with traditional skills. He has the authority to recommend ministers for new churches, and he wanted me to give him a few names.

As I listened to him, I thought again of the ways in which our Presbyterian system of calling and installing pastors is elegant, maddening, majestic, imprecise, well intentioned, and inefficient. In this sense, though each Protestant tradition has its own placement policies, all denominations share in the frustrations of matching the best pastoral candidates to the best ministry context for their skills. Nowhere is this frustration more evident than in the recent phenomenon among mainline denominations to begin new churches — and to develop strategies to support them.

A holy experiment is under way in a new church. Here is the beginning of a new faith community — with all its attendant institutional challenges — growing from within a gathering of people for whom participation in a religious institution (at least the institutional church) has in the past been unwanted, unknown, unwelcoming, or unsatisfying. A spiritual leader who can steer that ship through the storms of inception to the relatively calm waters of organizational maturity is not easy to identify, train, or support. The person who called me knew all this. What he did not know, however, was more critical to the long-term effectiveness of that new church. What he did not know forms the basis of this study.

For decades, as those inside the mainline denominations have watched the explosive growth of nondenominational church movements and the rise of megachurches and parachurches across the United States, questions have emerged concerning how the denominational church might be revitalized. (One of the leading voices in this conversation is the Gospel and Our Culture Network,[1] which focuses on the discussion of theological and spiritual issues.) At the same time, a new breed of pastors has emerged. These new pastors are not interested in ministry within existing churches, where the traditions, structures, and behavioral norms are already established. Instead, they wish to venture out into calls to start new churches. However, unlike their nondenominational counterparts, these pastors respect their denominational ties and maintain their denominational affiliations, though they may do so in a low-key style. Many of these pastors receive funding and other forms of tangible support from their denominations. Some operate, in fact, within the shadow of already existing churches within their denominations. These new-church pastors differ in many ways, but they are all united in their missional vision for their churches to be evangelizing communities that reach the unchurched. These pastors, following the apostolic call, target their new church for those who have never been affiliated with a church or whose church affiliations are so long lapsed (usually since childhood) that they are effectively unchurched. These pastors are not building new churches by cannibalizing the unhappy, the uninvolved, the misfits, or the marginal members of existing churches.

What sets these new churches apart — and what distinguishes the leaders who start them — are a range of variables that involve areas of spirituality, networking, support and training structures, evangeliza-

---

1. See www.gocn.org for their website. This home page of the network states that this network encourages a missionary encounter "of the gospel with the North American assumptions, perspectives, preferences, and practices."

tion, and leadership traits and skills. These variables form the primary focus of this study. What has been known until now is that not every pastor who begins a new church, even with multiple levels of support, succeeds. Sometimes the failure to thrive is attributable to failures within the placement systems. Churches often hire the candidate who wants the call rather than the one who can fulfill the call. In addition, the questionable validity of screening programs, which are also inconsistently applied, can result in the selection of the candidate who looks good on paper and who sounds good in the interview but who cannot perform adequately within the particular ministry context.

Denominational executives, including the one who called me that morning, understand that new-church development requires a specialized person. What they often do not understand is how the parameters for candidate selection might be applied and — specifically in new-church development — refined. The research represented in this book is designed to provide information about new churches, especially the leaders who are called to ministry within them. Specifically, these results are based on research addressing a constellation of variables that seem to contribute to the development of larger-membership new churches where a deepening commitment to Christ is lived out within a maturing community of faith among formerly unchurched persons.

This study does not focus on new-church-development (NCD) pastors in comparison to pastors who minister in traditional churches; and this is not a study of NCD pastors who fail in their calling. Instead, this is a study of new-church-founding pastors who are maintaining viable communities of faith; and it *is* a comparison of NCD pastors who lead larger-membership churches with NCD pastors who lead smaller churches. This study, then, provides much-needed information about the fragile and delicate nature of NCD leaders and the specific abilities, skills, and behaviors that characterize them. This study seeks to identify both the innate character traits and the learned church-development skills of extraordinary leaders who are meeting the sociological, missiological, theological, and ecclesiological challenges of these extraordinary times.

The Historical and Social Context of the NCD

After World War II a huge boom of new churches grew from within denominational loyalties and the legacies of Christendom. However, during the turbulent 1960s, membership in traditional mainline churches began to drop sharply, and the trend of decline continued throughout the second half of the twentieth century. The drop in membership closely followed the decline in new-church developments.[2] In addition, it was no longer simply a given that the children of Lutheran or Episcopalian or Presbyterian parents would themselves grow up to become members of their parents' church — or any church. Denominational leaders, increasingly concerned by the lack of adherence and loyalty, watched as the numbers of parachurches and nondenominational churches soared, many of which drew thousands of worshipers each Sunday. Furthermore, during the last few decades of the twentieth century, the advent of cable television and the Internet has spawned a new generation of "virtual" Christians, who seldom, if ever, worshiped in brick-and-mortar churches and had increasingly little inclination to do so. Denominational demarcations such as "Congregational" or "Reformed," which once signaled important distinctions of doctrine and polity, became flooded over by the tides of contemporary music, slick technology, and commanding presentations of a reductionist gospel message. Little "brand loyalty" remained among religious consumers. These factors, coupled with a sharp decline in the number of denominational new-church developments, contributed to staggering mainline membership losses.

During the mid- to late 1980s, several mainline church executives began to call for the expansion of church-planting efforts within their denominations. Their efforts did not create a boom in new-church planting as the twentieth century ended, but it did refocus some mainline energy and funding around the vision of starting new communities of faith. These executives offered support to clergy who expressed an interest in starting new churches; in addition, many executives be-

---

2. Stephen C. Compton, *Rekindling the Mainline: New Life through New Churches* (Bethesda, MD: Alban Institute, 2003). Compton discusses the issue of mainline membership decline in the latter half of the twentieth century and argues that the decline in new church starts is a significant contributing factor in membership loss.

gan to recruit new clergy for church-planting initiatives. These pastors were given financial support and, for the most part, a good deal of room for experimentation. They could begin meetings in their homes; they could contextualize the gospel for their neighborhood setting, take part in community affairs, start new programs, and focus on reaching the unchurched. The elbow room worked: many of these fledgling NCDs began to grow.

However, while some NCDs grew to include hundreds, even thousands of worshipers and began to develop into mature organizations, others hit plateaus and grew no further. Still others floundered and ultimately failed. Denominational leaders realized that the NCD strategy of a missionary church starting new churches was a good one and that, when the strategy worked fully, it worked well. They also discovered that when the strategy worked partially, it produced churches that were viable but often stalled in growth and became stunted in missional call. Finally, the denominational leaders began to discover that when an NCD flopped, that church was usually irretrievably lost.

The leaders of seven mainline denominations, having met in conferences since the late 1980s to discuss NCDs, began in the mid-1990s to envision a study that might capture needed information about the nature and workings of NCDs. Their interest was in NCD leadership: they had a collective hunch that NCD leaders tended to make or break a new church. The questions they had were: Which attributes, skills, abilities, and behaviors among pastoral leaders contributed to NCD success? Which were neutral to growth? And which impeded or hindered growth? These denominational leaders suspected that, despite all the denominational support systems and other variables a new church may have had going for it, it would not reach its full potential without appropriate leadership. In other words, no matter how much else was right, if the leader was wrong, the new church would be at best marginalized and would probably fail.

Recognizing the value such a study could provide, the seven denominational leaders designated some of their national funds to this study. Additional funding came from the Center for New Church Development at Columbia Theological Seminary. The denominational leaders also requested and received a Lilly Foundation Endowment Fund grant, which was entitled "NCD for the 21st Century." Those combined resources provided the funding for this study.

General Study Design and Applications

Seven mainline denominations participated in the study:

- Christian Reformed Church
- Episcopal Church
- Evangelical Lutheran Church in America
- Lutheran Church — Missouri Synod
- Presbyterian Church (USA)
- Reformed Church in America
- United Church of Christ

The study was designed to be a comprehensive investigation of new-church developers spanning the last two decades of the twentieth century. This book is the first of two volumes on NCD leadership: it accounts for data gathered from Euro-American NCD leaders; a second volume will focus on racial-ethnic NCD leaderships in five major ethnic groups found within the participating denominations. These groups correspond in ethnicity to denominational ethnic caucuses and, in some instances, to their national church development staffing. The five ethnic perspectives from which the second volume will explore leadership and NCD issues are: African-American, Hispanic, Asian, a specific subgroup of Asian (Korean), and Native American. The second volume will also further contextualize and address the multicultural complexities of new-church development as we enter the twenty-first century.

Data for this first volume are drawn from more than 700 Euro-American NCD pastors who responded to a survey. Out of these 700+ responders, more than sixty male and female founding pastors — most of whom were still serving the church they started — were gathered in focus groups that consisted of seven to ten pastors. The NCD study team selected these pastors for the focus groups because they considered them the most "effective" developers within their respective denominations. The study team used a narrow definition of "effectiveness" for the purposes of this study: "effective" leaders were defined as those who had formed the largest stable worshiping communities of faith with formerly unchurched persons.

Six of the seven denominations were represented in the focus groups (the seventh did not have a larger-membership congregation). The focus groups were structured to gather together pastors with roughly equal amounts of tenure in their respective NCDs. In other words, a pastor with fifteen years' experience with an NCD was placed in a focus group with other NCD pastors who had had comparable time and experience. In addition, the NCD pastors who participated in the focus groups completed a post-focus-group, open-ended written questionnaire.

The study team used both quantitative and qualitative analysis to sort the data. Outside evaluators and professional focus-group conveners also participated. The chapters and addenda of this book were written by four scholars who have had academic or pastoral experience (or both) in NCD work and other missiological endeavors within the mainline denominations represented.

In Chapter One, Darrell Guder, Henry Winters Luce Professor of Missional and Ecumenical Theology and dean at Princeton Theological Seminary, uses a telescopic lens to bring the data of the study into a universal overview. Taking the span of "Christendom" history as his starting point, Guder defines missional theology and makes the case for a thorough theological critique of new-church development as part of God's missionary activity. Rather than replicating the trappings of "Christendom," Guder challenges us to "rethink who we are and what we do from this central focus: the calling to be witnesses to God's love in Christ, in a particular place and in particular ways." He argues that many of these difficult post-Christendom trappings are evident in the underlying assumptions and motivations that guide these NCD pastors, and he calls the church to address these. Guder asks what, if any, conclusions can be drawn from the NCD study as it relates to the changing purpose and position of the church in post-Christendom America. He demonstrates the transitional nature of Christianity in this epoch and thus the importance for theological grounding as we seek to evangelize in the presence of a "complex religious demography."

Stan Wood, Ford Chair Associate Professor of Congregational Leadership and Evangelism at San Francisco Theological Seminary (and the project director for this study), uses three major streams of data to compile a trans-ecclesiastical profile of effective new-church-development pastors: the Founding Pastor Church Development Survey; transcripts of the six focus groups; and the post-focus-group questionnaire. Combing these strands, Wood considers in depth the mechanics, behaviors, attitudes, and vision that serve to make these NCD leaders effective in ministry contexts. Wood has, in essence, quantified some of the text so that the preponderance of various themes articulated by the pastors participating in this survey can be numerically weighted. This gives not only a description of the profile traits of effectiveness, but it rank-orders them. In Chapter Two, Wood introduces the profile and delineates the three profile traits that clustered significantly higher than all other traits, paying special attention to the highest-ranked trait, the "catalytic innovator." He concludes with a look at the meanings and interpretations that can be given to this research, especially its applicability to seminary communities and mid-level governing bodies within denominations.

Building on Chapter Two, Wood examines in Chapter Three a group of five traits that "constitute a separate but no less critical mix of gifts." These traits are quantitatively less robust, but they are no less critical to effectiveness. And while this second grouping of traits is important, it is a grouping that describes the aspects of effectiveness in ways less outwardly focused and more inwardly descriptive. These traits are less about "action" characteristics, but they map the inner world of the NCD pastor, including feelings, private habits, insights, and perspectives. Wood then points to longitudinal studies showing how extraordinary new-church developers change leadership styles over time. Finally, Wood compares the trans-ecclesiastical leadership profile points identified in these chapters with the twenty-four "Marks of Effective Ministry" delineated by Robert S. Hoyt in Addendum A.

In Chapter Four, Carl Dudley, professor emeritus at Hartford Seminary and a leader in the Hartford Institute for Religion Research, compares research from the "New Church Development for the 21st Century" study (the largest study ever conducted of new-church-development pastors) with research from the "Faith Communities Today" study (FACT) (the largest interfaith study ever conducted of North American congregations), a study Dudley directed. Both studies address the life of the church, though they approach their investigation in profoundly different ways. FACT begins by examining congregations themselves and then inferring from those data the character and mission of the congregational leader. The NCD study approaches it, in fact, from just the opposite direction. It begins by surveying the leaders and then inferring from their responses the nature and character of the congregations they served. The juxtaposition of these two survey instruments creates an interesting tension that guides the reader through the complex interlocking of the leaders and the led. While these studies are obviously not comparable, they are complementary. Dudley examines in depth what is known about the fascinating subset of NCD pastors through the larger lens of FACT.

In Chapter Five, Wood synthesizes the research from the survey and the scholarship of the four authors by asking what insights emerge from the analysis of the research survey. He concludes that the insights gained from this study will be invaluable to those who are concerned with the future of Christianity in general and with new-church development in particular.

In three excellent addenda, Robert S. Hoyt, formerly on the national staff of New Church Development for the Evangelical Lutheran Church in America, provides a rich description of the realities of new-church-development pastors as he allows us to hear these NCD pastors speak in their own words (Addenda A and B). Hoyt then shows how denominations might aid new-church development more effectively and how NCD pastors might serve as agents for transformation in mainline denominations (Addendum C).

This study shows how leaders in new-church development have used personality traits and acquired skills to start and sustain successful new-church developments. The data detail what is known about these leaders, what they say about themselves, and what factors seem to contribute to their effectiveness. The main outcome from the data is a constellation of traits that form much of the energy, direction, and personal style of these leaders. Identifying and understanding these traits are critical for those involved in developing new churches — and those who support and educate them.

This constellation of traits — the leadership profile — can also inform those who shape theological education. It may be that different kinds of recruitment and retention should be examined at the level of seminaries and theological schools, if those institutions are supportive of training people interested in this specialized form of ministry. The profile can also be used by denominations wishing to establish NCD training and assessment centers for interested clergy. Those who have the desire to enter into NCD work are often those most qualified to do it. However, the leadership traits are not instinctual; they depend on training, experience, and knowledge. Of course, those who are interested in ministry, and those who wonder whether an NCD might be a good fit for them and for their next call, can also use this information. Finally, this information can be useful to those already engaged in NCD work: the profile points can be touchstones to seek further training or to hone and emphasize leadership traits already expressed in ministry.

Like any study of this magnitude, it has its weaknesses. Those in executive positions within the participating mainline denominations created underlying assumptions that guided the research models and constructs; thus other constructs that may explain or account for effectiveness went unexplored. In addition, the study team assumed that NCD pastors all understood and applied the language used in the survey, in the focus groups, and in the post-focus-group questionnaire in the same way. For example, we assumed that those who indicated that they were "sharing their faith with the unchurched" meant roughly the same thing, though this sharing may have taken various forms. In addition, we conducted the quantitative analysis of the data by creating subgroups of the population according to church size. This method yielded robust results. But we did not try other ways of structuring the data, and alternate approaches may yet yield usable information that will be published in subsequent venues.

Our study conducted the qualitative analysis using the constant comparative method — with its attendant strengths and weaknesses. Furthermore, the study is a compilation of self-identified traits: we did not make observations, objective measurements, or rankings of the respondents, except for demarcations of church membership size as a guide to "effectiveness." Finally, this study is, in many ways, a retrospective. The NCD leaders relied on their memories to recount what they had done in the past, and their memories may or may not be reliable. We cannot discern, given the limitations of the design of this study, whether these memories capture all of the missional variables that led to church growth.

As with all studies of this nature, those of us involved in it have tried to capture in numbers and words something essentially elusive and mysterious: how the Holy Spirit grows and sustains Christ's church. In all matters of faith, we follow the mysteries as best we can. In the analysis that follows in this book, we have attempted to dissect and magnify the areas of the mystery that seem to have something as reasonable as cause and effect attached to them. This study suggests that there are particular leadership traits and skills expressed in NCD pastors who fulfill an apostolic calling.

Pastors who respond to this apostolic and missionary call may be recruited, trained, and nurtured as channels of God's grace. Yet it is God's gifting and power that make them extraordinary. About such leaders as these Paul writes: "If you only look at us, you might well miss the brightness. We carry this message around in the unadorned clay pots of our ordinary lives. That's to prevent anyone from confusing God's incomparable power with us."[3] It is toward the missional extension of God's kingdom as it grows and deepens, and it is for and in service to these NCD leaders, these "unadorned clay pot messengers," that we present this study.

Sabbath Hill   STAN WOOD
Atlanta, Georgia

---

3. II Corinthians 4:7 (Eugene Peterson, *The Message: The Bible in Contemporary Language*).

Chapter One

Leadership in New Congregations: New-Church Development from the Perspective of Missional Theology

Darrell L. Guder

My experience with pastors of new congregations has been primarily in the context of the Presbyterian Church (USA). I have had the opportunity to participate in a variety of events in which these colleagues were the constituency and their ministries were the subjects. Invariably, these encounters have proved exciting to me. Here was a group who had a sense of energy and direction in their ministry, people who were experiencing God at work in the lives of people as a congregation began to form, and people who knew themselves to be part of a dynamic process that was open-ended. The sense of commitment and the anticipation that God would be faithful were tangible. These encounters have encouraged and nourished me as a missiologist serving the church. That energy and excitement have certainly been reflected in the focus meetings that make up a significant part of the research base for this study, and they emerge in analytical emphases on vision, commitment, and energy.

Such encounters with new-church pastors are highly instructive because, in the concrete situations they face in forming new churches, these pastors are grappling with crucial theological issues related to the mission of the church in general. Because the life of such a congregation is just beginning, questions of purpose and mission — the "why" questions — dominate, while questions of maintenance and continuation are only beginning to surface. A new church can be compared to a missiological laboratory in which the opportunities and disappoint-ments, the steps forward and the steps backward, can be examined and dissected as though under a theological microscope.

Both the excitement of church pioneering and the analytical rich-ness of the new congregation are pervasively reflected in the data and interviews that constitute this NCD study. On page after page one en-counters men and women who are highly motivated by their minis-tries, who want to share what they are experiencing, and whose reports from their trenches lay out fascinating information about the church, its formation, its problems, and its distinctive characteristics within the North American context. One is impressed by and grateful for that energy and the insight. As we attempt to draw statistical conclusions from the collected data, especially with regard to the characteristics of "effective new church pastors," some things appear to be quite clearly established, whereas other important dimensions of the theological task appear to be more difficult. From the perspective of missional the-ology, this is not surprising. Since different readers may understand the term "missional theology" in different ways, I need to explain the theological lens through which I am responding to the findings of this study.

"Missional Theology" Defined

The theological discipline of *missiology,* which is little more than a cen-tury old, works on all the questions that cluster around the church and its mission. That means that this discipline gives attention to the bibli-cal foundations of mission, to the history of mission, to the doctrines that relate to mission, and to the practice of mission. It may seem strange that such important themes should have emerged as a formal theological discipline only in the late nineteenth century, but Western Christian theology has not really dealt with the theme of mission for most of our history. I will briefly summarize the reasons for this below; they are relevant for our investigation of missional perspectives on the leadership of new congregations.

We are now looking back on a process in the twentieth century in which a global or ecumenical concern for the theology of the church's mission emerged. For our purposes here, it will suffice to summarize the outcome of that long and fascinating process with regard to the understanding of the purpose and the function of the church in our Western contexts. Two major developments characterize the onward movement of Christianity in the twentieth century: 1) the emergence of the global church, and 2) the recession of Christianity in the Western world. On the one hand, "the great new fact of our time" (William Temple in 1942) was the fact that the modern missionary movement had resulted in the planting and growth of the church in all major cultural regions of the world. On the other hand, "Christendom" was over in the West. I use the term *Christendom* to describe the great tradition of Christianity in the West, rooted in the fourth-century decision by Constantine to give the Christian faith and church privileged status in his empire. His decision resulted in the emergence of the so-called "Christian civilization" of the West, in which virtually every area of life was shaped or affected by the Christian faith and the institutional church. In this discussion, I will cover the seventeen centuries since then, whose legacy we inherit, and will refer to them interchangeably as the "Christendom project" and the "Constantinian project."

One of the most important aspects of the Christendom project was the fact that the church became institutionalized as a geographical or territorial concept: it existed within the boundaries of the Christian states with which it was in partnership. Congregations were planted as the result of a monarch's decision and (usually) funding. Europe was divided into geographical parishes in the eighth century; the boundaries of a given area and the congregation of the church within that area became interchangeable. It was the task of the church to provide every one born and living within the parish boundaries the services of the Christian religion. In the long and complex process of Christendom, the *mission* of the church was replaced, largely, by the *maintenance* of the church as an institution providing religious services to the citizenry. Absent from this structure was either the theology or the language of mission. (There were, of course, exceptions, such as the monastic missionary movement, the evangelization of Ireland, and the Slavic mission of Saints Cyril and Methodius.) Whereas the biblical emphasis is on the people of God, on the community with its shared life and public witness, the preoccupation of Christendom had become the institution — with its structures, traditions, prerogatives, and wealth — and its own preservation.

3

Beginning with the Renaissance and the Reformation, this hegemonic structure began to fall apart, and by the end of the twentieth century it has disintegrated in virtually all of Western or North Atlantic cultures. During the twentieth century, as Christendom ebbed, the theological exploration of the church's mission emerged in new ways. If the church is no longer automatically guaranteed a privileged place in our secular societies, then what is the purpose, or the mission, of the church? *Why* should there be church, and *how* should there be church? How should the Christian church relate to a context that was once defined as Christian but cannot honestly be described as such anymore? How can the church's witness be authentic in cultures traumatized by two world wars, the Holocaust, and the nuclear age? How shall Christian witness be made in societies that have become avowedly secular and often antireligious? How does the church relate to new groupings described in this study as the "unchurched" or the "de-churched"? These are some of the fundamental questions that we must address when we think about the formation of new congregations in North America. And the theological process of the last decades has generated stimulating and provocative content to enrich this conversation.

A theological consensus has been formed regarding the church as it emerges from Christendom. The emphasis has shifted from the maintenance of the church (merely to continue what has been) to the recognition that the church is, and has been from its founding, missional by its very nature. Biblical studies have influenced the emergence of this consensus. What was the kind of community that Jesus intended? What was the purpose of Jesus' formation of the disciples? What kinds of communities were the apostles founding, and how did this communal formation continue in the epistles of the New Testament? Joined with the biblical enterprise has been a growing engagement of early Christian history, specifically the life and mission of the Christian movement before the beginning of the Constantinian project in the fourth century. Although we cannot return to that time and context, post-Christendom churches in the West are discovering important common ground with pre-Christendom churches. For example, both are minorities in highly diverse cultures; both often find themselves on the margins of their societies, and both face frequent hostility to the Christian witness. Together, the biblical and the historical resources are helping the church in the West reclaim its original purpose, which was laid out for it in the life, ministry, and message of Jesus.

The purpose of the church founded by Jesus and empowered by the Holy Spirit has been to continue the witness to the gospel for which Jesus called and equipped his disciples. Jesus' mission is rooted in God's mission, for the biblical testimony discloses that, from creation onward, God has been active and purposeful in the life and history of his creatures. His purpose has been the healing of the nations and the restoring of rebellious humanity to the relationship with God for which they were made — defined in Genesis 1 as their creation "in the image of God." Thus God's mission is being carried out as he calls, forms, and sends both a nation and chosen individuals to be agents of his work. That mission reaches its culmination in the incarnation of Jesus as God's Christ. As God the Father has sent the Son, so the Father and the Son send the church, empowered by the sent Holy Spirit. In the New Testament the church's mandate is defined as the following: "witness" (Luke-Acts), "proclaim the message" (Mark), "lead your life worthy of the calling with which you have been called" (Paul), "sending" (John), "disciple the nations" (Matthew). The church is thus a key instrument called and set aside by God for his saving and healing purposes for the world: "For God so loved the world. . . ." The purpose of God's work in history, as testified to throughout Scripture, is the healing of the nations, the reconciliation of a divided and sinful world, and the restoration of all things under God's rule. The vocation of God's people is to be a sign, foretaste, and instrument of God's inbreaking rule in Jesus Christ (Lesslie Newbigin, *Signs of the Kingdom*). God calls and sends a people to serve his purposes for the world. The word *mission* means "sending," and the church is the primary way in which God's sending is happening. This is fundamentally reflected in the findings of this study, which emphasize the centrality of evangelization and faith-sharing both as a priority of the pastor and as the shared task of all members.

This consensus that defines the church in terms of God's sending (the *missio Dei*) raises large questions for the practice of church formation. It requires that we do basic theology when we contemplate new-church development. The task is to ground the formation of a congregation within the larger understanding of God's mission, that is, the purpose for the calling, forming, and sending of Christian com-

munities as witnesses to and instruments of God's mission in a particular place. One way we can get at this kind of basic theological process
is to work through the following questions when we consider forming
a new congregation, while simultaneously confronting basic attitudes
inherited from Christendom that profoundly condition our church
communities:

1. How can the envisioned congregation define itself and its purpose as a concrete expression of God's mission? Put another way,
   how can a new congregation's DNA be missional from the very
   outset, centered on God's calling and sending?
2. How — in the initial process of congregational formation — can
   the difficult task of awareness-raising concerning the problematic legacy of Christendom be accomplished as a positive step
   that liberates a community for its mission in a post-Christian
   context today?
3. How can the envisioned congregation come to the shared conviction that God is at work making it into an *ecclesia,* a public assembly called together and set apart for a particular purpose — to be
   the concrete witness to God's saving purpose for the world here,
   in this particular place and at this particular time? How can this
   conviction counter the other inherited expectations about the
   purpose of the church (e.g., meeting members' needs, serving as a
   chaplain to society, and so forth) that obstruct missional focus
   and priority?
4. How can the envisioned congregation learn to understand itself
   as *kyriakon* (the Greek root of our word "church"), a people that
   belong to the Lord, a community that is the presence, the body of
   Christ in a particular place? How can this process alert a congregation to the reality of other "pretenders to lordship" that seek to
   take the church into their service, in unfaithfulness to the Jesus
   who is Christ and Lord?
5. How can the envisioned congregation understand its own life and
   action in terms of God's purposes — God's love for the world,
   God's healing of the world in the life, the death and resurrection
   of Jesus Christ, and God's appeal to the world in the gospel? How
   do we translate the theology of the *missio Dei* into the actual self-
   understanding and practices of a congregation?

This is what it means to speak of the church as missional by its very nature. As missional theology develops, doctrinal questions necessarily emerge as we continue this rethinking process. Such a process really means a "transformation of the mind" (Rom. 12:2) with regard to our understanding of who we are and what we do. There are compelling examples of such transformations actually at work, for example, when we read in a focus group how one new church

> ... made a decision early on that we were not going to be a membership congregation, that we were going to be a discipleship congregation.... We have focused on making disciples and covenanting to be a disciple. (FG 01-02)

> When you're talking priorities, what I had to do was constantly remind the people that we weren't building a church for ourselves. We weren't going to be this little group that's here just to take care of ourselves, but we were here to reach the community. (FG 87-89)

When congregations begin to think in this way, they are engaging in the kind of Christendom critique that is crucial for the formation of the missional church today. It is not an easy thing to reorient our thinking in such fundamental ways. In the last two centuries, while mission has again become a major theme because of the great modern missionary movement, too many churches think of mission as one of many programs of the church ("programs" refer to the activities we organize and fund; most "programs" carried out by Christendom churches focus on members and their needs). Mission is commonly understood as that which occurs when the church shifts its attention away from its members and internal activities. This kind of thinking is still prevalent: it is connected to the old Christendom idea that the West is Christian and hence that the mission of the church is to send missionaries to the unevangelized world beyond Western boundaries, to send those whose task is to bring the gospel and the benefits of Western civilization. One can still experience this kind of thinking when looking at the work of "mission committees" in congregations or considering the mind-set that governs so many "mission trips" that have become an important aspect of local ministry. One conclusion is inescapable: most Western churches are, by definition, not missional.

The challenge now is to rethink who we are and what we do from this central focus: the calling to be witnesses to God's love in Christ, in a particular place and in particular ways. Mission no longer begins when we cross a cultural or national boundary. In the context of a Western world that is radically secularized, mission defines the world in which new-church-development congregations now are planted and seek to minister. The mission field is *right here*. Being missional means being Christians who are

> . . . getting out into the community, connecting with the people who are there, finding out what the needs are, how the gospel is going to connect and speak to their lives and even having that shape the style of worship, finding what's going to connect with the community where the church is being planted — just getting out there in many different ways, many different times, many different styles and connecting with the community. (FG 87-02)

When a new church gathers for public worship, its mission has already been happening. It has happened in the countless encounters, invitations, and inquiries that have brought this particular community of people together. It now continues as the community gathers in response to God's call, is built up by the encounter with the gospel in word and sacrament, and is sent out to continue the mission "in the community."

> The people from this new congregation need to have a clear, strong sense of conviction that this is a God thing, that the church isn't going to shoot it down, or save it because it's growing, but that God has had his hand in this and called me and there's work to do here. So the expectation is that God is going to do something here. (FG 87-89)

Such faith communities are composed of Christians who live as a minority in a postmodern society and who must be, do, and speak their witness in a diverse and often very difficult mission field. This post-Christendom reality has profound theological and strategic implications for the entire enterprise of the formation of new congregations. It sends us back to Scripture and the church's apostolic foundations to learn, in surprising ways, what we are called to be and do as the witnessing community of Christ. In particular, this missional understanding of our common calling broadens our vision to see the world God loves and into which God is sending his people. It means that a congregation's members know that "they are not end users of God's grace. [They are] not spiritual cul-de-sacs" (FG 90-93).

In particular, this post-Christendom missional context requires that we consider how every dimension of our corporate life serves or fails to serve the missional vocation of the church. It no longer makes theological sense to make a division between the internal, member-serving aspects of the church and the external, world-serving aspects of her ministry. What we do when we gather is directly and essentially related to what we do when we are scattered in the world. How we live as a community is the first and most visible form of our witness. Our worship, our fellowship, our decision-making, our management of money and property, our conduct before a watching world — as well as our formation of each other for our missional vocation — all are directly related to our mandate to be Christ's missional people. To put it in doctrinal language, our corporate ethics have become a primary theme of our evangelization, our missional witness in a post-Christian world.

Theological Implications for Congregational Formation in North America

This "paradigm shift" that now defines Western Christianity has obvious implications for the theology and practice of the planting and forming of new congregations. These implications will guide our thinking as we assess the data and findings of this study of new church leadership. However, it is not an easy process, because we find ourselves constantly reflecting the mindset and attitudes of a Christendom project that is, in fact, over. We've already referred to such a holdover when speaking of the way that "missions" are still regarded in many congregations and even denominations as the church's "foreign enterprise," or its way of spending money on causes other than the congregation's own life.

In the decision-making process that leads to the plan to start a new church, this paradigm shift requires that we investigate whether a project is missional or maintenance. That is, do we initiate such a project in order to provide the religious services of a particular tradition or denomination in a geographic area? Is our motivation to meet the religious needs of a population of potential "church consumers"? Or do we engage in a discernment process that recognizes truly missional reasons for the formation of such a community, a work of God's Spirit preparing the way for such a community, and guides the initial steps in its formation? It is no easy challenge to sort out the motives and subtle mindsets at work when we go about new-church development. The systems within which we work often make it difficult, as one pastor in a focus group vividly describes them:

> Our denominational leaders said, "Now go out in the community and find our denominational people that have moved out there and develop this church." So there wasn't a whole lot of getting to know the community, getting to know the area. It was more of, okay, find those who have that background, whether they are lukewarm or whatever, make sure you get out there, develop a men's club, a women's club, a choir. And after you have all the stuff together, then you have planted a church. It took me a while to get past that, to get to the point of saying, What are we here for? (FG 87-89)

This candid description of the systemic challenges we inherit from Christendom leads, very appropriately, to the basic theological question: "What are we here for?" In the process of developing a new church, the pastor-evangelist poses the crucial question that a missional theologian will also raise in reviewing the findings of this study. To get at the core issues, it is useful to divide it into two questions: First, why initiate a Christian congregation in a particular place? Second, how should such an initiating process take place?

Why Form a New Congregation?

The response to this question in the New Testament context was clear: the formation of faith communities was an act of obedience to our Lord's mandates. It was the way God's healing purposes were to be witnessed to and the way the inbreaking rule of God in Christ was to be demonstrated before a watching world. The apostolic missionaries were "sent out" by Jesus (sending = mission) and empowered by his Spirit to be witnesses whom God would draw together into communities to continue their witness to Christ, and thus to continue his mission. The purpose of their discipleship, their training with Jesus, was that they should become apostles (or "sent-out ones"); the result of their sending was to be the formation of communities in which this gospel was actually at work, transforming and healing people, creating a witness to the hope and certainty of God's promised salvation. Thus the New Testament is largely focused on the continuing formation of such communities. These written testimonies were formulated for already believing and testifying congregations, for the purpose of continuing their formation and equipping them for their mission. Their sense of who they were and what they were there for was defined by Jesus' words in John: "As my Father has sent me, so I send you" (the "you" is plural). Their life as a community was defined by the Pauline imperative, a pervasive theme from the early to the late Pauline literature: "Lead your life worthy of the calling with which you [plural] have been called" (Eph. 4:1; see 1 Thess. 2:11-12; Col. 1:10; Phil. 1:27). Their focus was not so much on themselves as it was on Christ, his message, and the world he came to heal and to save.

The challenge we face today, in a post-Christendom world, is coming to terms with the complicated and, in many ways, quite marvelous history that precedes us. We are the heirs of God's faithfulness through over seventeen centuries of the "Constantinian project." Nothing can eradicate the profound legacy of faithfulness and gospel witness that has passed this good news along from generation to generation and into our own time. We would not have the scriptural witness were it not for the faithful transmission and translation of that written witness as evidence of this faithfulness. But as I have noted above, Christendom as a social and political structure is over, and we now have to face the mixed results of the project. These results are particularly problematic for the task of new-church formation (though they can also be seen as a wonderful opportunity). Not only did Christendom develop the parish mindset described above, which has made the church into a territorial reality (summarized by the common term "local church"), but it has also shaped the message that we believe and proclaim. We can only briefly summarize these results, but their implications are enormous for the task confronting the Christian church in this Western, post-Christendom context.

Every aspect of our faith has been shaped in some way by the Christendom project. The church, as an institution, has come to be identified with Western culture: people speak of the United States or of European countries as "Christian nations," though the statistics of actual Christian commitment and involvement certainly belie such a claim. There is a subtle assumption at work that the Western church really represents the kingdom of God as Christ intended it and that our traditions and institutions constitute "normative Christianity." (This has been a very problematic attitude in the formation of non-Western churches in the missionary movement.)

And the gospel itself has been affected. We have come to understand the gospel, more and more, as primarily focusing on the salvation of the individual: his or her status of "savedness" with its implications for eternal life. I describe this process as "reductionistic."[1] I use that term to point out that the emphasis on personal salvation is not wrong but too small, too narrow — a reduction of the gospel from its world-focus to an individual focus. This is what the focus-group pastor correctly criticized as the idea that Christians are "end-users of God's grace . . . spiritual cul-de-sacs." A corollary to this reductionistic focus has been to reduce our understanding of the church's mandate to one of "salvation management": to provide the means to its members for the reception, maintenance, and eventual realization of the gift of God's promised salvation. Again, this is not wrong; it is simply too small, and it eventually distorts the gospel. It leaves out our theological understanding of the gospel and the church as described in the New Testament. That is, it effectively underrates the central emphasis on God's reign, breaking in now in Jesus Christ, and the certain outcome of what God is doing to heal creation. There is a clear and compelling emphasis in Scripture on God's inbreaking reign and the concomitant "sentness" of the church to be the witness to the world of God's healing love for all.

The further implication of this reduction of the gospel message is the powerful — yet often very subtle — expectation that the congrega-

---

1. On the theme of "reductionism," see Darrell Guder, *The Continuing Conversion of the Church* (Grand Rapids: Wm. B. Eerdmans, 2000).

tion in a particular place exists largely to meet the religious needs of its members, customarily through the activities of worship, fellowship, pastoral care, and tangible acts of support and help. Again, all of these activities are essential aspects of the church's mandate. But when churches focus primarily on the benefits that accrue to church members when they avail themselves of membership, and when this focus detracts from or substitutes for the scriptural mandates to nurture the missional call of the church, then a fateful and anti-missional reductionism is at work.

This reductionism was at home in the parish system of Christendom. Mission, or "outreach," when it was done, was largely the work of specialized groups who moved outside the boundaries of established Christianity. A major example was the monastic orders in the Middle Ages, which not only rebelled against the spiritual weakness of the church but also moved across many borders to evangelize among pagan cultures such as the Irish, the Scots, the Saxons, and the Slavs. For Protestants, this understanding of mission was nourished by the impressive activity of the missionary societies that, since the late eighteenth century, moved out from the North Atlantic to proclaim the gospel in unevangelized areas and to plant churches there. Here at home our missionary activities consisted of raising money for those abroad and of recruiting young men and women to carry this work forward.

The political and social development of North America greatly complicates the picture. Over two centuries ago, our political and social order was profoundly influenced by the decision to "disestablish the Christian church," that is, to end the centuries-old pattern of church-state partnership that Europeans brought across the Atlantic to America. It is obvious, however, that the attitudes and mindsets of Christendom persist in American society. People still define themselves as "Christian" even if they are not active in a church. "God Bless America" is one of America's most beloved songs. Compared to most other industrialized nations of the world, American's populace exhibits a higher level of religious activity and interest, though much of it is distinct from any concrete link to a congregation or an organized church life.

This has meant that a combination of Christendom and post-Christendom motives has informed the process of congregational formation. The parish system as a territorial strategy continues: the churches arising out of European traditions (we call them "mainline

churches") continue to envision their congregations as a denominational system that provides their religious services to their constituencies through geographical strategies. These "geographical strategies"
are somewhat blurred by the mobility of American society, of course.
Baptists will drive past many Baptist churches to attend the church of
their choice. However, in the main, Baptist, Congregational, Episcopal,
Lutheran, Methodist, Presbyterian, Orthodox, and Roman Catholic denominational leaders have traditionally established parishes wherever
the presence of a demographically determined constituency seemed to
suggest such a tradition would be welcome and viable in the vicinity.
They demographically identify the region; they assess potential membership; they measure the active interest in having such a congregation;
and if the data prove conclusive, they initiate the formation of such a
congregation to draw together that constituency and to meet its needs.

This process is unavoidably intermixed, however, with a distinctly
American element of entrepreneurialism. When the church, very early
on, became an independent and private organization with no state support, it began to develop forms of fund-raising and management that
relied on the energies of volunteers. That volunteerism has brought
into the life of the church enormous innovation, energy, and commitment. It has also, as a functioning institution within a larger culture,
mirrored the entrepreneurial economic system. Furthermore, it has integrated the values of the entrepreneurial system into the life of the
church — with its emphasis on growth, success, and numbers.

Therefore, all North American churches are, by legal and cultural
mandate, private and voluntary organizations that are dependent on
the support and involvement of their members. The constitutional
principle that makes establishment impossible effectively forces the
church to focus on its own maintenance as a priority. Hence, when any
denomination initiates a congregation, it must do so with a view to the
financial viability of this new organization. The financial pressure ex-
erted on the new congregation combines with the awareness that a significant proportion of the American public is not, or is no longer,
"churched." At this point, definitions begin to break down. Many "unchurched" Americans self-identify as Christians simply because their
personal values seem to align with the teachings of Jesus (as they understand them) without any allegiance to a community of faith. Conversely, many formerly "churched" Christians may be inactive within

faith communities simply because their personal worship needs are not engaged and met in existing communities of faith. The proliferation of "American indigenous churches," whose shape and practices differ greatly from inherited traditions, is yet another indication of the difficulty we now have in defining what is, in fact, a church.

Many Christians are aware, in some sense, of the fact that America is a mission field. They know that fewer people are going to church today, that members of their families no longer go to church, that there is little Christian influence in the public media, and that religion is largely banished from secular school systems. Many older Christians are painfully aware that their adult children do not practice the faith in which they were raised. Church members are aware that there are people to be reached with the gospel and to be drawn into a particular congregation who have little or no rooting in a particular Christendom tradition. This is often a puzzling tension: on the one hand, there is the widespread assumption that ours is a Christian society (although this seems to describe more a kind of Christianized culture than a committed confession of faith); on the other hand, the evidence of secularism is on all sides, and the public voice and role of the mainline churches have clearly declined in the last decades. For many who are part of the religious right wing of our society, this requires energetic efforts to restore some of the trappings of a faded Christendom (e.g., prayer in schools, the Ten Commandments in courtrooms, and so forth). Our society is, in fact, made up of a confusing variety of orientations and attitudes toward the Christendom legacy that still profoundly shape our national life.

Many Americans are Christians; the polls would indicate that a majority of Americans define themselves as such. And there are clearly thousands of Christian congregations actively engaged in ministry. Many congregations are grappling with the missional challenge of our post-Christian world. There is real ferment, and there is even a "continuing conversion" to missional vocation.[2] Other churches appear to exist primarily for the maintenance of their denominational traditions;

---

2. See *Continuing Conversion* and, in general, the publications of the Gospel and Our Culture Network, especially George Hunsberger and Craig Van Gelder, eds., *The Church Between Gospel and Culture: The Emerging Mission in North America* (Grand Rapids: Wm. B. Eerdmans, 1996); Darrell L. Guder, ed., *Missional Church: A Vision for the Sending of the Church in North America* (Grand Rapids: Wm. B. Eerdmans, 1998).

they seem to be struggling. Many people still relate to a congregation as "cultural Christians": that is, they self-identify as Christians because they are not something else religiously, and because they believe that their society is still basically a Christian one. They are often described as "Christmas and Easter church-goers." Others have a memory of Christian identity: it is the tradition of their parents or grandparents, and it may resurface when they want a church wedding or a baptism for their children. This may also serve as a point of re-entry into the life of faith. At the other end of the spectrum are the growing numbers of churches that have no visible ties to Christendom traditions but are emerging out of modern culture in unconventional forms. These churches are often growing dynamically. As we have already noted, they may appropriately be described as "American indigenous churches," and they include many so-called megachurches, as well as a staggering diversity of house churches, specialized fellowships, and genuinely new formations of Christian community.

Parallel to them — and often equally vital — are the growing numbers of ethnically and culturally distinctive Christian churches that have come to this country on the waves of immigration. These represent one of the most fascinating and challenging aspects of the complexity of the North American cultural context, and they constitute a significant part of the strategies of many of the denominations in this study. These new churches demonstrate the fundamental translatability of the gospel that is an essential aspect of contemporary missional thought.[3] In many denominations, these new churches represent the most vital form of new congregational formation, reflecting the demographics and the growing numbers of immigrant communities. On the one hand, these churches are a response to the need of such constituencies to worship in their own language and to function as communities of mutual cultural support. On the other hand, they are also frequently a pioneering form of outreach to unevangelized populations, in which Christians in a particular ethnicity reach out to non-Christians in their communities and invite them to become followers of Jesus Christ.[4] The theological chal-

3. On the translatability of the gospel, see especially Lamin Sanneh, *Translating the Message: The Missionary Impact on Culture* (Maryknoll, NY: Orbis, 1989); Stephen Bevans, *Models of Contextual Theology* (Maryknoll, NY: Orbis, 1992).

4. The second volume of this study will provide data on racial and ethnic new-church-development pastors.

lenge with which such ethnic movements contend is the tension between the desire and demands for ethnic ministry "to their own" and their missional vocation to North American culture beyond their own ethnicity. These congregations often struggle with the pressure to serve primarily as a cultural home base for their members in the difficult context of North America, a motive that can become just as theologically reductionistic as any inherited motive from Christendom. The second- and third-generation congregations of such ethnic constituencies are especially engaged by these tensions. It is interesting to see, for example, how many English-speaking Korean congregations are now grappling with their mission to the larger North American context and, in the process, becoming self-critical of a narrowly defined cultural mandate.[5]

Turning to the "unchurched" in the American mission field, it is notable that we are not dealing with a homogeneous mass of pagans but a much more diverse mixture of attitudes, resistances, and opportunities for mission. There are, for instance, "inoculated" post-Christendom people who have rejected that legacy for a variety of reasons. They represent perhaps the most difficult constituency to reach: they are most resistant to the gospel because of past experience, and they are the most skeptical about the efforts of an institutional church to recruit them. There are the religious experimenters, people who combine strands of their Christian tradition with elements of the occult, Eastern religions, "New Age," and their own ideas. (An example of this was cited in a *New York Times* article [September 19, 2003] that described a new movement, "The Church of Crafts," which finds religious fulfillment in shared creative activity.) For many of them, the traditional congregation will not be innovative, creative, and unconventional enough.

Another sizeable and growing component of the American population is genuinely pagan. They have no idea what the gospel is all about; they have probably never been inside a church; and they are dominant in some parts of the country, especially on the west coast. These people constitute, in many ways, the greatest opportunity for

5. For an introduction to this discussion within the Korean Presbyterian network, see Guder, "Christ: Answer to the World," in *Proceedings of the National Korean Presbyterian Council,* July 2-5, 2002 (Princeton, NJ, Louisville, KY: Presbyterian Church [U.S.A.], 2002).

Christian outreach, because there is little need to correct or overcome misconceptions about the gospel and the mission of the church. Many of the congregations participating in this study have discovered and are engaging this mission field, as one pastor testifies:

> I found myself for the first time preaching the basics of the faith because I had one young man who came, and I said, "Let us pray the prayer our Lord taught us." And he came up afterwards and he said, "I didn't know that that prayer was what the Lord taught. This is the first time I've been in worship." And I realized that people, the seekers, are coming, and they've got a hunger and they've got a thirst. . . . (FG 94-96)

Along with the growing numbers of truly post-Christian Americans, we see the growing communities of adherents of the other major world religions, all relatively recent arrivals on our shores. Every American city is witnessing the building of mosques, Hindu temples, and Buddhist shrines as the other world religions are becoming part of our society.

There is a corresponding spectrum of approaches to this task of reaching the unchurched, which is formed by the way one understands the gospel and its claims. One can approach the "unchurched" from a reductionist understanding of Christian vocation, summarized by the idea that "being a Christian is the same as being a church member." This results largely in organizational recruitment for reasons that may or may not have much to do with personal conviction or biblically defined faith. As I have just noted, people will still join churches for basically cultural reasons, reflecting deeply embedded but reductionist understandings of what the Christian gospel and the church are really all about. They will seek out churches for the programs that meet their needs, the facilities and activities that attract their children, or the social activities that complement their lifestyle. And along with this spectrum of approaches are perceptions of the church that have to do with social and ethical concerns for society: that the church functions as a prophetic voice calling for change or acting on behalf of those who are victimized by society or dealt with unjustly. The summons in this kind of prophetic church is to become part of a faith community that is seeking to carry out the important social dimensions of the gospel.

In addition, there is a more "evangelical" option. One can also view much of the American population as unevangelized, that is, as lacking any identifiable personal conviction, any real sense of knowing and following Christ. The church planter can thus see his or her role as that of an evangelist who reaches out to people with an invitation to become a follower of Christ and a member of the church. In specific instances, the self-understanding of those initiating new congregations will often reflect a mixture of various emphases along this spectrum.

This complexity of religious demography presents the strategist for church extension or development with an opportunity: congregations may be formed both to draw together already existing constituencies ("find all the Presbyterians in the area") and to reach out to people who do not consciously relate to the traditions of Christendom any longer. To use ecclesiastical language, the new church may serve to "reaffirm personal faith" or to lead to the "profession of personal faith," with the result that a congregation is formed. It is significant that, in the design of the NCD study, the theme of evangelism is statistically weighty (e.g., Survey Q-22-28, 30f, 31a), and it was constantly emphasized in the focus groups. The awareness of evangelism as a core element of successful growth within the new church is certainly an important factor in the strategizing of many who set out to plant a congregation.

Given the rapid secularization of much of North America in urban areas and on the west coast, the strategy may shift more toward the evangelization of individuals with no conscious denominational affinity. This connects with the emergence in North America, already briefly noted above, of a great variety of churches that are themselves consciously post-Christendom — that is, denominations (though many don't want to use that term) that are genuinely reflective of and rooted in American culture (or better, cultures). The forms and beliefs of these movements, though they are all dependent in some way on the Christendom project, are shaped much more by North American culture and by the great variety of strategies to translate the gospel (however reductionistically) into that culture. The result is an enormous variety of "church styles," which are reflected in organizational structures, patterns of leadership, church architecture, worship styles, and approaches to theology.

The missiologist, looking at this American variety of churches, sees here an important demonstration that the gospel[6] is fundamentally capable of being translated into every cultural or subcultural context. That there is no established "American" way to be church is not only an outworking of the political separation of church and state but also a reflection of the fact that North America is itself profoundly multicultural. It is also becoming progressively clearer that older denominational patterns of the church are not necessarily binding. It is interesting to note that, in the focus groups of the NCD study, issues of denominational loyalty or conformity to denominational patterns were frequently played down or even discounted as now strategically irrelevant in reaching out to unchurched Americans.

> They [the founding group of members] would not allow us to put a sign on the property that would say something like "future home of the Presbyterian church" or anything like that. So even when we started building, people didn't know what kind of church it was. In a sense it became more of a community church, so that Protestant people — Lutherans, Methodists, Presbyterians, everybody across the board — kind of saw it as a Protestant church. So they came to it even though we were certainly Presbyterian in format, in style, and in worship; but we didn't keep putting ourselves out there as the Presbyterian Church. We were putting ourselves out there as the church for the people. (FG 87-89)

Cultural translation and appeal are frequently seen as a greater priority than the maintenance of denominational names and signs.

A theological analysis of this highly varied scene is exceptionally difficult. Most of the analytical work tends to focus on empirical standards for "success," which have to do with numbers, growth, funding, public attractiveness, and services and programs provided. There is an unmistakable element of cultural influence in the religious enterprise in America. While there are fluid guidelines shaping the partnership of church and state, more rigid partnership boundaries have been forged between the marketplace and the church. At the same time, many of those interviewed exhibited a remarkable awareness of these market pressures and the temptations toward consumerism rather than theo-

---

6. See note 3.

logical integrity. One pastor spoke candidly to this theme, referring particularly to the risks that face a large congregation:

> I think one concern today for large churches is that we must be very careful that we not become five miles wide and one inch deep, as the saying has it. And there are accusations that you can cave in to a consumer mentality, that we're serving up some kind of, you know, religious entertainment that attracts people and really isn't significant. I think that probably, to some degree, we all struggle with that in terms of integrity and in terms of hopefully being really faithful to the calling of the gospel. (FG 87-89)

The calling to serious discipleship, as formation for missional vocation, is the alternative to "marketplace churchianity," which is such a temptation in the North American context:

> We have the marks of discipleship, and that has made a huge difference. I think it's brought people deeper into the workings of the ministry of the church rather than thinking, "I can come in, sign this piece of paper, I'm a member, and now I can sit back and relax." It's not a health club where you pay your dues and come whenever you feel like it. We're looking for partners, not members. (FG 01-02)

New churches are not founded in a cultural vacuum in North America, and so the challenge, from the perspective of missional theology, is always to grapple with the ambiguity of our context and its impact on the ways we think and decide. The countercultural thrust of the Christian community aims to transform the "religious consumer" into the "missional partner":

> You get individual members involved in ministries touching the needs of the people in the community. You turn people loose. It's that priesthood of all believers concept that's been around. You turn them loose in ministries, and you give them permission to care. You don't put them on a board. You don't put them on a committee. You don't make an usher out of them. You make a minister out of them and put them in situations where they're dealing with life issues of normal human beings. And that draws. (FG 87-89)

In summary, the missional theology of the church raises difficult and important questions about why new congregations are founded in our post-Christendom context. This theological approach, which necessarily works biblically, historically, doctrinally, and practically, recognizes that the process of congregational formation is a complex mixture of major motives and factors, some of which are in tension with each other. On the one hand, there is the powerful Christendom legacy, which focuses on the maintenance or conservation of Christian traditions in a variety of ways. We must recognize this as part of our Christian vocation, as it acknowledges and claims God's faithfulness over the centuries despite the ambiguous history of Western Christianity. But at the same time, this recognition can often result in an understanding of the church that emphasizes servicing people's religious needs, often fulfilling religious roles "assigned" by our cultural context (e.g., "chaplain to society," "vendor of religious services," "curator of beautiful traditions"), and preserving denominational and institutional structures as ends in themselves. The theological nuances within the maintenance approach can vary: they may range from various questionable forms of "cultural Christianity," to the role of the church as an agency for needed social uplift or for prophetic challenges to social inequities, to a primary focus on "servicing the saved" in a particular tradition. Or, to use other theological lingo, one can "maintain" the church for good liberal, moderate, or evangelical reasons. A good deal of new congregational formation is primarily shaped by this maintenance motive.

The other major cluster of motives can be defined as *missional*. The governing theological understanding is the "mission of God" and the missional nature of the church as I have outlined it above. The effect is to concentrate on calling people to follow Christ and become part of his witnessing people. Linked with that motive is the necessary analysis of the North American context as a difficult mission field that requires new and innovative forms of gospel translation. The life and purpose of such faith communities is understood as witness, as demonstration of the inbreaking reign of God. Such communities are beginning, at least in a preliminary way, to question their Christendom legacy, and they are open to asking hard questions about the meaning of the reign of God in Christ and what it means for the way they carry out the vocation of every Christian congregation in its particular context.

The conversations with the focus groups reveal that these motives are largely mixed in most denominational church starts. Maintenance and mission are both present as powerful themes, and there is often remarkable awareness of this tension. Various strategies are being tested to address this tension, many of them leading toward greater freedom in cultural translation and, with that, intentionally less emphasis on traditional identity and practices. In view of all the data and the great variety of strategies and experiences with new congregational formation, the missional theologian continues to ask: Why initiate a congregation in a particular place? How does the church discern the Spirit's leading there? Are demographics a theologically responsible method of discernment? Is the presence of an initiating *community* — that is, a group of people who are willing to be drawn together to begin a new Christian congregation of a particular tradition — a clue to discern God's leading? Or can it be that a particular *individual* feels called to initiate a congregation for ministry and mission in a particular place? Does the Spirit work through the regional strategizing of a denominational agency?

On the basis of the impressive array of anecdotal evidence (more than statistical on this point), it can be said that all of these options, and undoubtedly others as well, are possible indicators that the Spirit is forming a community of faith. Discernment arises, following the New Testament, out of a complex texture of doors opening and doors closing, people responding to the invitation and people rejecting it, the Spirit's prodding individuals and groups to take first steps and to await God's affirmation and the opening up of further possibilities. What is important, theologically speaking, is the purpose for the formation of such communities. It must always be for the initiation of gospel witness in particular places and ways, which is the continuation of the original apostolic mandate that has formed the church since Pentecost.

Maintenance in a Christendom mode, if it is given as the sole reason to start a church, is not an acceptable rationale for church formation from the perspective of missional theology. At the same time, the Christendom legacy is not only an unavoidable cultural component with which a community must struggle but also a rich resource. One must understand the Christendom context that shapes us, even when forming a church that consciously moves outside and beyond it. One can find in this long story much that inspires and guides the Christian community today (one example is the growing interest in Celtic spirituality), as well as much that calls for repentance and conversion.

The research, both statistical and anecdotal, does stress the pivotal importance of forming communities that intentionally seek out and welcome those who are not yet believers, but those in whose lives God is at work, and whose call is being prepared before the evangelizing pastor or neighbor initiates a conversation. Inviting people to become followers of Jesus Christ must continue to be the central thrust of all ministry, the priority of the founding pastor-evangelist:

> [Convener]: Complete this sentence for me, and you've been saying it over again, but let's say the same words again: "An effective founder must be passionate about . . ."
>
> [Respondent 1]: "the lost"
>
> [Respondent 2]: "the gospel"
>
> [Respondent 3]: "seeking . . . seeking the lost, to me, that's what the Bible is doing"
>
> [Respondent 4]: "helping people meet God — that's why we're here"
>
> [Respondent 5]: "There needs to be a deep, deep passion for God, because that will really show in the worship service. People will not sense the presence of God if the pastor is not expecting or does not want God to show up, you know. So those passions, I think those passions are placed there by the Holy Spirit. And passion for God and passion for people and passion for the lost is probably a real top priority . . . passion." (FG 94-96)

The concern of missional theology is that this central commitment to evangelization should itself be defined by the following conviction: the very call to follow Christ is a call to become a fisher of people, an invitation to join God's mission and become part of the witness to the inbreaking reign of God. That thrust will help congregations and their leaders avoid the reductionism that separates the benefits of the gospel from the missional calling of those who are being evangelized.[7]

7. On this problem of the dichotomy between "benefits" and "mission," see Guder, *Be My Witnesses: The Church's Mission, Message, and Messengers* (Grand Rapids: Wm. B. Eerdmans, 1985; Academic Renewal Press: www.arpress.com, 2003).

How Shall New Congregations be Formed?

The design of this research project answers this question by focusing on the leadership that initiates new congregations. The project looks for the characteristics of the effective planter of a new congregation and tests several basic hypotheses regarding such persons. This process is justified in missional theology. There is no biblical example of the "spontaneous generation" of a witnessing congregation. All congregational formation takes places as a response to apostolic witness, to the translating and demonstrating of the gospel, coupled with an invitation to become a follower of Jesus and a part of his missional community. In the New Testament the evangelist is always a church planter. The strategy is not just the salvation of individuals but also the formation of witnessing churches. Scripture itself is written for and to communities of faith, addressing their continuing formation for witness in their specific contexts. The missional nature of the church is inextricably linked with the apostolic generation of each congregation.

This understanding of missional vocation is attested to in a variety of ways in this study, especially in the testimonies to a sense of personal calling to plant a congregation, the drive that could not be expressed in any other way (see Survey Q-36c, 37b, 37d), and the sense of awe and thanksgiving that these pastors often show as they look back on their very diverse personal faith and ministry journeys. It is also apparent that this sense of vocation was linked to an awareness that one had to proceed by discovering others in a location who had a similar desire to be part of the formation of a community of faith (Survey Q-36e). To put it theologically, the apostolic messenger had to discern those people whom God had placed in readiness for this initiation. This necessary discernment may have emerged from "requests or inquiries from local residents of [a] denomination" (Survey Q-9); however, it was likely that very few of those who initially responded to the initiative to start a new congregation had significant previous Christian formation (survey Q-29). One of the paradoxes of the Christendom legacy in North America is the fact that people still regard our context as Christian, yet biblical and theological illiteracy are widespread — if not the dominant characteristic of the population. The practical implementation of this discernment of potential lay leadership is reflected in the variety of ways the survey shows that lay formation took place: "teaching or leading Bible study" (Survey Q-30b); "leadership development" (Survey Q-30d); "small-group development" (Survey Q-30g). One can argue that all of this bears the imprint of the basic New Testament patterns of congregational formation:

- The apostolic messenger (often itself a small team, e.g., Paul, Sylvanus, and Timothy) presents the gospel story and the invitation to respond, discovering the people God has been preparing to become part of the apostolic mission.
- A small community of respondents emerges with Spirit-empowered faith.
- The apostolic formation begins with personal instruction, epistles, and (later) written gospels, and revisitation.
- Leadership is appointed to guide and continue the formation and practice of the congregation.
- The communities grow as the witness is translated into and becomes visible within a specific context.
- Communities struggle with internal discord and experience "continuing conversion" as their formation for witness advances through such struggles.
- Communities experience resistance and even persecution as their testimony is seen as threatening in that context.
- Their witness continues as they foster the outreach that leads to the formation of further witnessing congregations.

Basic to this understanding of the formation of such communities is the role of apostolic ministry. Proclamation moves immediately to community formation, which then continues both personally and in the form of Scripture. These written testimonies emerge in the early church as the Spirit-empowered instrument God uses for the continuing formation of missional congregations. The key to their interpretation, then, is missional. We must constantly ask of these written testimonies how they formed God's people for their missional vocation then, and how they do so today (this is the theme of "missional hermeneutics," the scope of which obviously goes far beyond the appropriate work of this chapter). It is important to note, however, that the biblical record should function, in the contemporary process, as both the model and the agency for the continuing formation of such evangelists and the communities that emerge from their ministries.

Looking Back and Thinking Forward

The ancient wisdom of the church that the calling to ordered ministry is a process with a dual dynamic is certainly affirmed by both the statistical data and the focus groups of this study. Such a calling is made up of both an internal sense of call and an external acknowledgment of gifts for ministry by others. The sense of personal calling is essential, but not enough on its own. There must be an ecclesial process of examination and affirmation that such a calling is joined by the gifts for ministry as seen and experienced by others. This study has generated insights that should be helpful as the process for the selection of church leaders continues to be refined by denominational agencies. These findings also have implications for seminary training. There is, however, more work to be done with regard to both calling and gifting for the evangelization of the post-Christendom church and its conversion to its missional mandate in this changed and changing context of North America.

It is interesting that this research instrument generates little data with regard to the entire area of spiritual formation and disciplines on the part of the founding pastor (with the possible exception of Survey Q-31g, "having a lay group which regularly prayed with me," and the underlying spiritual discipline of worship and sermon preparation). By contrast, this theme emerges in the focus groups with considerable emphasis, and the post-focus-group questionnaire abundantly documents the concern for "abiding faith in God," for "a deep and sincere faith," and for intentional spiritual disciplines. This comment is typical of many: "I would tell mission planters that first they need to have a prayer life. That's essential. And then be aware of your own purpose as you seek God's purpose and a process for carrying God's purpose out" (FG 01-02). Reflecting on the focus-group conversation regarding spiritual formation, Robert S. Hoyt says:

> These leaders were clear about the source of power in their lives. They started the day with prayer and continued in prayer. The con-

stant challenge to overcome was not to rely on themselves but give in to what God was doing to lead them in the development of their ministry. By making room for God in their daily lives they achieved balance and renewal.[8]

In another study in which I have participated,[9] there is reference to the importance of corporate prayer in the missional transformation of a congregation. This was connected to the finding that such congregations were profoundly shaped by their encounters with biblical teaching and study as the primary way in which they were experiencing missional formation. In this study, it is also sobering to see how little either denominational agencies or institutions of theological education appear to have contributed to this process (Survey Q-14-16; somewhat more encouraging is Survey Q-32). None of the questions refers directly to the substance of the theological formation of a new-church pastor; in fact, theology is an almost unmentioned theme in the study, although certainly implied at points. One wonders how the missional rereading of our theological disciplines might prepare leaders in different ways for the formation of new witnessing communities. It is refreshing to read pastors' comments emphasizing their continuing commitment to theological discipline — reading regularly and working with what they gained in seminary. But these pastors are also understandably critical of seminaries' deficiencies in realistically preparing them for the challenges they have to face.[10]

The study as a whole constitutes a challenge to those engaged in missional theology to acknowledge that the work is clearly only in its beginning stages. Although there is a growing body of theological work that directly relates to the missional nature of the church and the need for conversion to that calling in the West (see especially the entire leg-

8. Robert S. Hoyt, Addenda A-C in the present volume.

9. A study of "patterns of missional transformation in congregations," conducted by the Gospel and Our Culture Network, in Lois Barrett, ed., *Treasure in Clay Jars* (Grand Rapids: Wm. B. Eerdmans, 2003).

10. "I didn't do well in the seminary because I didn't get theology, and I wasn't sure I should be a pastor. And the men and a few women at that time who were getting into these deep theological debates — I thought, okay, I don't belong here because they are the ones who should be the pastors. I know this is a rap on seminary, but you come out with a head full of theology and very little of what we're talking about, very little practicality. I didn't get the theology and somehow I'm doing okay" (FG 87-89).

acy of Lesslie Newbigin, as one among many), the translation of this theological work into the concrete formation of pastoral and lay leaders of the church has only just begun. Both the findings and the omissions of this study are an extremely helpful contribution to the work of missional theology. In the meantime, the actual work of new congregations will continue to generate insights, challenges, and understandings that will shape the formation of missional theology. What Martin Kähler articulated over a century ago, "Mission is the mother of theology," is still true.[11]

---

11. Martin Kähler, "Mission und Theologie," in Heinzgünter Frohnes, ed., *Schriften zu Christologie und Mission* (Munich: Christian Kaiser Verlag, 1971), p. 190.

Chapter Two

The Tier-One
Characteristics of an Extraordinary
New-Church-Development Pastor

H. STANLEY WOOD

Throughout her history, the church has had men and women whose passion has been to take the message of the gospel to the unchurched. This zeal exists in every generation, in both genders, among varying age groups, and in every corner of the world. How such passion comes to exist is a holy mystery that is linked to the graciousness of the Holy Spirit working within the human heart. Regardless of the subtlety of the design, understanding the formation of such passion may always elude theologians. However, there is a great difference between the formation of this passion and its results, which, when expressed in measurable and concrete forms, yield to examination.

This chapter focuses on one important examination of measurable results: the identification of a trans-ecclesiastical leadership profile of the most effective new-church-development (NCD) pastors in seven mainline Protestant churches. What traits and spiritual gifts best describe an effective NCD pastor? Are there leadership qualities that transcend the denominational differences that exist among the seven denominations participating in this study? If part of what it means to be "effective" stems from the growth and maintenance of a large-member congregation, then how might population shifts and spurts account for church growth?

In order to preserve the integrity of the "NCD for the 21st Century" study, special care and scrutiny were given to this final question.

The senior executives from these seven denominations wanted the data about effective NCD pastors to reflect more than simply the "effectiveness" of a pastor who stumbled into a boomtown. They agreed that targeting hot spots of population growth and calling a pastor to start a new congregation at that location did not lead to automatic membership growth in an NCD — or to automatic pastoral effectiveness. In other words, inside every boomtown there is a level playing field of opportunity for ministry. While several denominations may send their best and brightest to do ministry in the boomtown, the proportional rates of growth will be decided by the leadership traits and skills of the NCD pastors who take the calls. Some NCD pastors will be more "effective," relative to the congregational size of other churches in the same area, than will other NCD pastors. Lyle Schaller underscores this point:

> The record makes it abundantly clear that population increases do not automatically produce membership growth for churches. *A more realistic term would be to label these communities experiencing a rapid increase in population as "high competition areas."* In most of them other people also are planting new churches. A reasonable assumption is that at least a few of these new missions will have the benefit of exceptionally competent ministers. *This usually means they [these new missions] provide a highly competitive environment for both the existing congregations and also for those new missions with average or slightly above average quality pastors.* It is not surprising to find disappointed denominational leaders who had expected rapid growth in that new mission they planted in what is really a highly competitive ecclesiastical environment. [emphasis added][1]

All the denominational executives in this study had experienced the disappointment Schaller identifies. For this reason, although many factors influence new congregations and their growth, understanding the pastoral leadership became a core research path for the executive team. If measurable, identifiable, and perhaps educable traits exist in effective NCD pastors across all denominational lines, then an analysis of their styles and traits would provide those committed to the mission

---

1. Lyle Schaller, *44 Questions for Church Planters* (Nashville: Abingdon Press, 1991), p. 42.

of the church a valuable touchstone for identifying and nurturing these pastors and others who wish to enter this challenging field.

All of the denominations surveyed used ordained clergy for pastoral leadership in church planting. Thus the executive and research teams chose to focus on pastoral leadership because they believed it to be one of the key factors (perhaps the ascendant factor among all salient ones) in rapid and sustained membership growth. This chapter presents a profile of new-church pastors who provided extraordinary leadership between 1980 and the close of the twentieth century. In defining pastoral leadership, we used the terms "extraordinary" or "effective" to mean: 1) those pastors who started and sustained new churches that achieved the highest membership growth within their respective denominations; and 2) those pastors who were able to attract and assimilate formerly unchurched persons into active church membership.[2] These effective NCD pastors were then gathered into focus groups for in-depth qualitative study, and the categories of this profile arise from

2. The researcher recognizes the theological limitation of defining church development effectiveness within the narrow confines of attracting and assimilating formerly unchurched people. Effective church development is not just focused on the mission of the church to those who are unchurched or under-churched. Indeed, the writer locates the assumptions about the effective church development as being broadly placed in Christ's sending of the church into mission. This focus of sending is found in Christ's so-called Great Commission, namely the missionary task of "making new disciples" (Matt. 28:18-20). The mission is understood to be larger than the Great Commission and is interpreted as being rooted in the very nature of God made known in the Trinity and expressed in the Reformed theological contours of *missio Dei*, a theological concept coined by Karl Barth to express the multiple facets of mission. For an explanation of the many expressions of effective church mission, see David Bosch, *Transforming Mission Paradigm Shifts in the Theology of Mission* (Maryknoll, NY: Orbis,, 1991), section III. However, the research task identifying a trans-ecclesiastical profile of an NCD pastor was sharply focused on those pastors who showed leadership that was effective in attracting and assimilating formerly unchurched persons. This sharp focus was chosen since it presented a statistically verifiable method for identifying effective NCD pastors. All participating denominations had statistically similar means for tracking new-member congregational growth through monitoring the inclusion of "new believers," "adult baptisms," and "renewed believers" who joined the church but who had no church letter to transfer onto a membership roll. Hence the NCD pastors providing leadership in congregations with high membership growth of formerly unchurched persons were targeted for qualitative study. Those targeted for study were founding pastors who continued as the senior or head-of-staff pastors in the congregations they planted.

the data collected within each focus group.[3] We invited the pastors to respond to two questions:

1. As you think about the role of the founding church pastor as leader, please identify several leadership competencies or functions/behaviors needed in the early stage of new-church development.

2. Does the leadership needed in later stages of a church's development differ from the early stage? If so, how?

The research team used qualitative analysis to create categories in the profile based on the pastors' responses to these questions. No profile can adequately capture the subtle nuances of phrasing and inflection found in each pastor's comments; rather, this profile is a composite of the leadership traits, behaviors, and spiritual gifts found in these extraordinary developers.

Each of the two charts provided below shows the responses (ranked by percentages) to the two questions. That is, as the profile categories emerged from the total data collected, each category was ranked by the number of times it appeared in the comments of the participants; hence, each chart shows the percentage of responses by profile categories.[4]

---

3. Research methodology is based on the "Constant Comparative Method" of data analysis as outlined by Sharon B. Merriam in *Qualitative Research and Case Study Applications in Education*, 2nd ed. (San Francisco: Jossey Bass, 1998), chapters 8-9.

> "Unlike experimental designs in which validity and reliability are accounted for before the investigation, rigor in a qualitative research derives from the researcher's presence, the nature of the interaction between researcher and participants, the triangulation of data, the interpretation of perceptions, and rich thick description" (Merriam, p. 151).

> "The basic strategy of the method is to do just what its name implies — constantly compare. The researcher begins with a particular incident from an interview, field notes, or document and compares it with another incident in the same set of data or in another set. These comparisons lead to tentative categories that are then compared to each other and to other instances. Comparisons are constantly made within and between levels of conceptualization until a theory is formulated" (Merriam, p. 159).

4. Merriam says that "moving beyond basic description to the next level of analysis, the challenge is to construct categories or themes that capture some recurring pat-

In response to the first question (asking participants to reflect on leadership competencies and functions needed in the early stages of new-church development), the pastors ranked the following as critical:

Early Stage of New-Church Development
(First 7 Years)

Tier 1	Catalytic innovator	20%
	Vibrant faith in God	15%
	Visionary/vision caster	13%
		48%
Tier 2	Empowering leadership	8%
	Passion for people	7%
	Personal and relational health	7%
	Passion for faith-sharing	7%
	Inspiring preaching and worship	7%
		36%
Tier 3	Administrative skills	5%
	Other categories (7)[5]	12%
		17%

Note: The total of the percentages exceeds 100 because of rounding.

The second question addressed changes in leadership styles as the church organization matures. What additional or different skills are required to pastor a church in its early maturing years? Pastors ranked the following as necessary skills for sustained leadership:

---

tern that cuts across 'the preponderance' of the data . . . . Devising categories is largely an intuitive process, but it is also systematic and informed by the study's purpose, the investigator's orientation and knowledge, and the meanings made explicit by the participants themselves" (p. 179).

5. "Other category" accounts for seven single-digit percent characterizations, namely, "humility/patience" 3%, "authenticity" 2%, "ties to a learning community" 2% (only NCD pastors in the mid- to late 1990s remarked on mentorship and national training events, which parenthetically relates to when most of the surveyed denominations began mentorship and national training event programs), "denominational support" 2%, "care for community" 1%, "experience (in an NCD)" 1%, "sense of humor" 1%.

Later Stages of New-Church Development
(Years 8 Through 20)

Tier 1	Ability to change leadership styles	35%
	Empowering leadership	24%
	Understanding change dynamics	13%
	Vision casting	8%
		80%
Tier 2	No change	7%
	Other categories (5)[6]	13%
		20%

Discussion of the Profile Categories

These responses seem to indicate that effective church developers believe:

1. There is a unique constellation of competencies that exist among effective leaders of NCD congregations within the first seven years of ministry.
2. Furthermore, there is a different and equally important set of competencies that exist in the following years.

Founding a new church and providing leadership as the church develops are dynamic processes that change as the congregation moves from inception toward maturity. As churches are planted and mature, they develop from an initial movement driven by a founding pastor to an increasingly complex organization driven by multiple lay and pastoral leaders. It would seem likely that the skills, abilities, and gifts of pastors would vary dramatically at different times during the maturation process of the new congregation.

During the first seven years of new-church development, NCD

---

6. "Other categories" includes five single-digit percentage categories, namely, "ties to a learning community" 4% (see note 5 for definition), "administrative skills" 4%, "personal care" 2%, "discipleship training" 2%, and "humility" 1%.

pastors' responses clustered around what we called the "catalytic innovator." An operational definition of this term is given below. What is important about the facets of the "catalytic innovator" is simply this: the pastors interviewed believe that these are the most critical skills of an NCD pastor in the first seven years of new-church development. The aspects of a "catalytic innovator" are captured below:

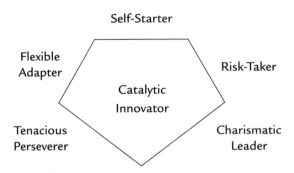

Self-Starter

Flexible Adapter

Risk-Taker

Catalytic Innovator

Tenacious Perseverer

Charismatic Leader

Catalytic Innovator

A catalytic innovator, in the simplest dictionary definition, is "somebody or something that makes a change happen or brings about an event," someone who introduces "a new way of doing something."[7] In fact, the word "innovator" comes from the Latin word *innovare*, which means "to renew." It is thus important to note that the term "catalytic innovator" is a coinage: it is intended to describe multiple symbiotic traits. The term itself arises from data gathered from the post-focus-group written questionnaire:

> As you think about the role of the founding church pastor as leader, identify several leadership competencies or functions/behaviors needed in the early stage of new-church development.[8]

7. The catalytic innovator is the top profile trait, making up 20 percent of the NCD pastors' self-identification of the "leadership competencies or functions/behaviors needed in the early stage of new-church development" (first post-focus-group question asked to all developers).

8. Catalytic innovator had 53 responses, or 20 percent of all answers written.

The Constant Comparative Method identified five sub-aspects of a catalytic innovator from the qualitative data: these aspects arose from data describing a constellation of skills, behaviors, and ideas that extraordinary new-church developers value. These five aspects, taken together, are crucial competencies for success in the early years of ministry. Listed below are the five aspects of the catalytic innovator:

- Charismatic leader
- Tenacious perseverer
- Risk-taker
- Flexible adapter
- Self-starter

Each of these aspects arose from the data analysis of pastors' comments. The following are the broad descriptors that shaped the five categories, with notations as to which groups emphasized what. The exact wording of the pastors' phrases can be read in tabular form below, followed by a more complete discussion of each aspect. Again, these data must be viewed through the lens of the success of these pastors. According to the most "extraordinary" NCD pastors, the following spiritual gifts, skills, and competencies are necessary in the early stages (first seven years) of new church ministry:

Subcategory 1: charismatic leader
- Entrepreneurial (1990-1993) (1997-2000)
- Entrepreneurial skills: hang in there, make it work, figure it out (1997-2000)
- Entrepreneurial/risk-taking (1994-1996)
- Charisma and enthusiasm (1997-2000)
- Effective public presence/leadership dynamic (2001-2002)
- Boldness (1987-2002)
- Charisma (1987-2002)
- Total commitment to building a community of faith, whatever it takes (2001-2002)
- Faith-/perseverance-/hope-filled (1997-2000)
- Model for the people (2001-2002)
- Strong sense of call to church development (2001-2002)

Subcategory 2: tenacious perseverer
- Courage of convictions (1987-2002)
- Commitment: forget the trial or test of interest; go in with an affirmed "We're here!" (1987-2002)
- Is willing to do whatever it takes/whatever God asks (1987-1989)
- Tenacity (1997-2000) (1994-1996)
- Persevere (1987-2002)
- Is committed for the long haul (1987-1989)
- Persistence (1987-2002)
- Perseverance — not a quitter (1994-1996)

Subcategory 3: risk-taker
- Risk-taker (1987-2002) (1994-1996) (1997-2000)
- Courage (1987-2002) (1997-2000)
- Ability to take risks and be flexible (1997-2000)
- Should be a creative, risk-taking person who deals with conflict (1994-1996)
- Resilient (1997-2000)
- Willing to try many things, willing to fail (1997-2000)

Subcategory 4: flexible adapter
- Willing to embrace change (1997-2000)
- Handles/lives with ambiguity (1990-1993)
- A problem solver; does not let problems intimidate him/her, but recognizes the opportunities therein (1987-1989)
- Comfort with ambiguity (1990-1993)
- Problem solver (1987-2002)
- Flexibility (1987-1989) (1987-2002) (1997-2000)
- Flexibility — gifts, ideas, but no preconceived notions (1987-1989)
- Flexible within a definite vision that God has given (1994-1996)
- Flexible, adaptable — while holding up the vision for this NCD and helping people to come on board; "buys into" that broad vision (1994-1996)
- Flexibility, but also the commitment to keep the vision (1987-2002)
- Adapt with laughter (1997-2000)
- Adaptable (1987-2002)
- Ability to change and willingness to change (1990-1993)

Subcategory 5: self-starter

- Ability to learn, make mistakes, reinvent self (1997-2000)
- Willing to be engaged with this emerging church at every level of its development (1987-1989)
- Creator, initiator, developer (1994-1996)
- Willing to make mistakes (1997-2000)
- Self-starter, hard worker (2001-2002)
- Good self-starter (1990-1993)
- Self-starter (1994-1996) (1987-2002)
- Self-starter/ self-feeder (1994-1996)

What follows is a discussion of each of the aspects of the catalytic innovator in more complete detail.[9] If the most effective NCD pastors are catalysts, if they "got the right things done" in an innovative way,[10] then certain questions necessarily follow: How did this process happen? How do catalytic innovators create something from nothing? How do catalytic innovators function?

First Subcategory: Charismatic Leader

Effective NCD pastors are charismatic leaders. Their leadership is not exercised in a social or religious vacuum; they live and traffic in an ambiguous moral and social climate that is not always hospitable to their vision. Put another way, NCD pastors work in a "competitive market," where forces of apathy and disconnection work to keep the unchurched out of a dynamic faith community. Charismatic leaders sharply hone their skills against the forces of this "market." It is perhaps not surprising, therefore, that effective NCD pastors freely describe themselves as "entrepreneurs." One NCD pastor summed up a discussion about entrepreneurship in the church by saying, "That's a word — 'entrepreneur' — that, in the last five or six years, I've not been afraid to use around clergy" (FG 90-93).

9. The amplification of the five descriptors will marshal databases of the quantitative survey and the focus group findings.

10. Peter Drucker discovered that top executives do not have "effective personality," which may differ in temperament and interests; however, they have in common the "ability to get the right things done" (*Effective Executive* [New York: Harper Collins, 1966], p. 22).

The fear of using the word "entrepreneur" around clergy has deep roots. There are many in the church who view entrepreneurship as antithetical to ministry. This stems in part from the unflattering association of the term with a greedy and manipulative materialism; when it is understood as such, few would want to link it with the mission of Christ. However, when understood to mean the creation of a faith community with all the multifaceted administrative, bureaucratic, and complex roles necessary to sustain such a fellowship, entrepreneurship becomes, in a sense, synonymous with an acceptable and mature form of missionary zeal. These are entrepreneurs who want to do more than share the good news of Christ with disparate, unconnected individuals; they seek to bind those individuals together in a committed union of service and fellowship. They seek to experience the worship celebration of many individuals dynamically drawn into one community — rooted in one place, serving one Lord.

The term "catalytic innovator" captures the entrepreneur's bold style of work; and again, it emphasizes that the work of the innovator is not done in a vacuum. Catalytic innovators are involved in more than just working; they also lead. And they carry out this leadership in the same bold manner as in their work. It could be linked, as in Romans, to the spiritual gift of "leadership."[11]

One developer described his leadership this way: "You have to stick your neck out, and you have to be willing to take the rejection (or whatever you're going to get), because it's out there" (FG 87-02). Another leader spoke of the inherent dilemma of this charismatic expression of leadership: a bold leadership style is a "double-edged sword because there is a danger. I think you have to be a people person. You have to have some sense of charisma that's going to attract people. But the

---

11. The spiritual gift and role of leadership is recorded in one of the biblical lists of spiritual gifts located in Romans 12:4-8. A leader is defined as one who leads with "diligence" (12:8c) and "according to the grace" (12:6) given to the leader. Church-development leadership is the ability to see a goal and *motivate* the body of Christ to fulfill the goal. Leadership may be a God-given ability, or it may be developed as a learnable "skill." In the context of this study, leadership is the ability to "pass on" to others God's vision and call. William Easum puts it this way: "New life comes to us on its way to someone else: If we pass it on to others, we blossom and grow; if we keep it to ourselves, we wither and die" (Easum, *Dancing with Dinosaurs* [Nashville: Abington, 1994], p. 18).

negative side of that is this: Are people coming to church because of you or because of Jesus Christ?" (FG 01-02).

What are the nuances of this form of bold spiritual leadership? How do leaders temper the strength of their gifts to meet those whose lives are filled with the addictive mediocrity of the culture around them? The catalytic innovator's leadership style is doubtless dynamic, but it also has to be delicate and judiciously managed. They describe themselves as developing the role of resident leader, which one developer described as the "driver's seat" in a universe of spiritual captivity. These catalytic innovators walk in a world where the gospel must be boldly proclaimed if people are to be called to freedom in Christ. The following quote captures the rigors of this style of leadership:

> One thing that I really think has to be there — and I think we're not really saying it, or haven't said it yet — is something along the lines of "you have to lead." You're in the driver's seat. And while you're an equipper and a facilitator, while you're all of the other kinds of things, there comes this time in the dark night of your own soul and your own relationship with God. God has given you the vision of setting the people free. You're the one. You've got to go into Pharaoh's camp. You have to hold up the standard. You have to go up on the mountain and you have to lead. And that's the function of being in that driver's seat. (FG 97-00)

John Maxwell comments on the difference between management and leadership: "True leaders recognize a difference between leaders and managers. Managers are maintainers, tending to rely on systems and controls. Leaders are innovators and creators who rely on people. Creative ideas become reality when people who are in a position to act catch the vision of their innovative leader."[12] This is a helpful distinction toward understanding the different kinds of success these catalytic innovators pursue. Of course, a growing membership is important to them; the numbers, in a real sense, count. They are in touch with bottom-line management issues. But that is not the whole scope of their vision of ministry. These are leaders who are also capable, in the midst of counting membership numbers and budgetary dollars, of

12. John Maxwell, *Developing the Leader Within You* (Nashville: Thomas Nelson Press, 1995), p. 27.

keeping in touch with the top issues. They never lose sight of the grand call of God in their lives. In other words, they are able to discern God's dream in "Pharaoh's camp" and are diligent to carry it out. Leadership is spiritually rooted in giftedness and is behaviorally rooted in a learned skill. Leaders hone the gift and learn the skill by asking insightful and appropriate questions. One of Maxwell's insightful and appropriate questions for leaders is: "Am I building a people — or am I building a dream and using people to do it?"[13]

In summary, charismatic leadership serves as a subcategory of catalytic innovator. It suggests that these leaders possess both the traits of the entrepreneur (which must be translated into more palatable language for some in the church) and the nuances of a spiritual gift. Underscoring all the traits and gifts is an enthusiastic and committed dependence on God's guidance. These leaders are actively engaged in building a new community of faith, and they are dependent on God's leadership. One leader summed up charismatic leadership this way:

> I would say what God is going to do *to* you is more important than what God is going to do *through* you. . . . That's been my experience. God has done things in me that are more important than what he's doing through me. In other words, he's going to bring the church together in spite of my faults or my strengths or my *gifts as a leader*. He's going to accomplish what he wants to accomplish. But I have to be faithful to him, to my family, to the simple things of obedience. He's called me to be faithful [italics added for emphasis]. (FG 01-02)

Second Subcategory: Tenacious Perseverer

A catalytic innovator is a tenacious perseverer. Like workers in every field, these developers go through times of ease and times of difficulty; despite the times, though, they persist in growing and building the church. These are leaders who often grow and build in the darkness of uncharted territory. They must have enough agility and intelligence to

---

13. Maxwell, *Developing the Leader,* p. 127.

keep the vision of where they are going, and they must continue to nurture a fledgling organization regardless of whether the environment is favorable or adverse. Hence, among these leaders there is a pioneer entrepreneurial spirit coupled with tenacious perseverance. One described the trait this way:

> You got to figure out how to get from here to there, and you got to stay with it when things aren't going right, and you just got to see it through. Many other pastors in an established church will say, "We're not going in that direction." (FG 97-00)

Others described the trait as "doggedness": "You just keep going" (FG 97-00). "[You] just make hard decisions" (FG 94-96).

Part of that doggedness is developed in the crucible of tough decisions. For example, it takes tenacity of spirit to face the pastoral conflict of letting go of founding members. Frequently, those who initially joined the new church in a spirit of love and adventure may eventually become dissatisfied with the new directions. They may want their ideas to dominate. Or they may want to keep the new church small, and keep themselves as key players in it. This can run counter to the missional direction set in motion by the organizing pastor. Several of the developers talked about this phenomenon and the resulting conflict that can erupt from it.

Remarking about the rewards of persevering in a missional direction, one developer said, "It's amazing how much freedom there is in being able to say good-bye to someone" (FG 90-93). Setting innovative missional directions for the relatively fragile life of a newly forming congregation is an "attitude that [the NCD pastor] brings to [NCD ministry] that leads [the members] over the slumps and valleys and keeps them going" (FG 87-89). Staying the missional course of faithful witness takes directional perseverance. Rick Warren compares this trait to surfing: "When a surfer wipes out because he didn't ride the wave correctly, he doesn't give up surfing. He paddles back out into the ocean to wait for the next wave God sends in. One thing I've learned about successful surfers: they are persistent."[14] The same can be said of highly effective NCD pastors: they are indefatigable; they are tenacious; they persevere.

14. Rick Warren, *The Purpose-Driven Church* (Grand Rapids: Zondervan, 1995), p. 22.

Third Subcategory: Risk-Taker

A catalytic innovator is a risk-taker. Of course, it's true that all entrepreneurs who begin new businesses are risk-takers; furthermore, many
leaders — in all kinds of organizations — are risk-takers. Traditionally,
clergy are considered mild risk-takers who manage the boundaries of
risk well. However, an effective NCD pastor takes risks with exceptional
energy and when the stakes are exceptionally high. On the downside of
every risk is the sharp edge of failure. One NCD pastor summed up the
incredible edginess of risk-taking as follows:

> At every step along the way, we were saying, How in the world are we
> ever going to do this? How are we going to fund this? We knew if we
> didn't do that, we would never get to where we needed to go. We
> just decided to step out and faith it. We knew it was the right thing
> to do. We're just going to build the plane while we're flying it. (FG
> 97-00)

Going it on faith alone brings two unexpected spheres for potential — and public — failure. First, NCD pastors are frequently under tremendous denominational pressure: every success brings denominational visibility. Second, as membership growth occurs, NCD pastors
become accountable for developing a larger-membership church. Several commented on the pressure of denominational visibility:

> The denomination was supporting us, and we knew that after two
> years we were going to have to be self-reliant. Fear plays a role more
> than anything. . . . It's not being afraid to risk. We screwed up a lot.
> But, to me, the failure is falling and not getting back up — and not
> learning anything. We've had some expensive learning experiences,
> but that's all I see them as. (FG 87-89)

Commenting on the pressure to build, one church developer said,
"I think, in being a planter, it's a real risk-taking kind of thing. A lot of
us came from bigger churches. We're going from one church to another
church" (FG 94-96).

Being willing to make mistakes, to learn from them, and to go
right on taking risks is God-rooted. Risk-taking is defined by one
planter as the ability to "connect back with God after you fail. . . . That

allows you to get back in the ministry or make the connections back into the life of the church again. If you can't connect in with God after you've failed, you've got no strength or power to keep going in the ministry" (FG 97-00).

In essence, failure comes with the territory in the effective NCD church. But managing the failure without becoming paralyzed or fearful is the hallmark of effective leaders. They recognize that, no matter how strong their vision or belief, no matter how talented the team around them, failure may be the result of any venture. Knowing this, they risk again and again. These leaders are risk-takers in church development. They invite emerging congregational leadership into a risk-taking adventure that has high peaks and low valleys.

Defining a catalytic innovator as a risk-taker is not unique among leaders; but it is indicative of a small band of leaders in every generation who thrive on risk, who live for it, who dive in. Writing of Abraham Lincoln and this band of what he calls "genuine leaders," Donald Phillips says:

> Genuine leaders such as Abraham Lincoln are not only instruments of change, they are catalysts for change. . . . Lincoln effected the change needed by being extraordinarily decisive and by creating an atmosphere of entrepreneurship that fostered innovative techniques. In so doing, he not only got things moving, he also gained commitment from a wide array of individuals who were excited at the prospect of seeing their ideas implemented. . . . Lincoln's obsessive quest for results tended to create a climate for risk taking and innovation. Inevitably there were failures, but Lincoln had great tolerance for failure because he knew that if his generals were not making mistakes they were not moving.[15]

Effective NCD leaders, according to this definition, serve as "genuine leaders." They create an environment where risk-taking is invited and where intention weighs more heavily than failure. Failure is a lesson in what not to do next time. It is not an end; it is a means toward discovery in the adventure of faithful congregational witness.

---

15. Donald T. Phillips, *Lincoln on Leadership: Executive Strategies for Tough Times* (New York: Warner Books, 1992), pp. 138-139.

Fourth Subcategory: Flexible Adapter

The catalytic innovator is a flexible adapter. An adapter is a skilled change agent who is agile and flexible with people and their agendas. To adapt is "to change, or change something, to suit different conditions or different purpose; to adjust, to make or become used to a new environment or different conditions."[16] Flexibility in the adapting process of congregational formation brings a double measure of change: it underscores the importance of leadership that is wedded to ultimate goals — not to processes, people, or short-term objectives.

NCD pastors largely work with formerly unchurched people. These are people who do not bring to the doorway of the church a sense of ecclesiastical decorum, tradition, or politics. One described this amorphous gel of intentions as "real wet cement. It's real loose. . . . And yet it starts to harden quickly in those first several years. And sometimes the hardening agent is growth, because growth changes things" (FG 94-96). Adapting not only involves changing processes and plans; it involves changing paradigms as well. "We live in a culture that says, 'Here's how you do that.' The only thing I was looking for was flexibility. That's the key, I think, for all of us. You have to be flexible as you go, and you have to be willing to change. . . ."(FG 97-00).

Flexible adapters may change. They may interact with unchurched people and create nontraditional organizational start-up situations, but they are not completely compromising. Being flexible does not allow for a diminished or compromised gospel focus:

> I decided after the first day . . . to throw away my agenda. . . . I was knocking on doors entirely; that was not the approach I wanted to take. I really wanted to be open to looking for the gospel in the people I was encountering. . . . I was going to let the Spirit dictate where things went. (FG 87-02)

NCD pastors who come into the new church with their own agendas quickly learn the limits of their own flexibility. It isn't easy to give up a cherished agenda or a favorite process or happy memories of what worked before. But NCDs must adapt to the new environment they

16. *Microsoft Encarta College Dictionary,* p. 15.

serve; they must analyze where they are and who surrounds them; and they must develop a ministry that meets the needs of the new environment in appropriate and exciting ways. Missiologists have a good term for the analysis of a new-church setting or environment: they refer to "context," by which they mean the analysis of environment in order to contextualize the gospel.[17]

In a very real sense, effective NCD pastors are flexible about the medium of the message, but not about the message itself. They will adapt to varying cultural contours, but they are immovable concerning the ultimate truths of the gospel message. They flow into different contexts with the same unchanging call. Part of the skill of adaptation involves the analysis of the community or missionary context. Once they understand the context, they have to have the skill necessary to make adaptive changes concerning where and how the church will be called to be faithful:

> The flexibility of adjusting to, you know, the stages of ministry is also important in the beginning. And I think that one of the biggest problems of people who go into new church starts is [this]: they come in with kind of an agenda of what they want to do. And I think that you have to come into a new church situation with no agenda and let the community that gathers and the community in which you live set the agenda for you. (FG 87-89)

Frequently, flexibility spills over into the private lives of these pastors. The boundaries between work and home become blurred — not on rare occasions, but as part of the warp and woof of ordinary life. Often these pastors' homes doubled as church meeting places: "[Church was] our home the first year and a half, until we moved into the strip mall. We did everything other than worship. I mean, people had keys to our front door" (FG 87-02). Being able to transform adversity into opportunity while remaining flexible with personal space was also important and, interestingly, simultaneous. On this same theme, another pastor says: "After sixteen years I think one of the things that I've tried to learn to do is to be positively transformed by adversity, to grow with

---

17. For example, see Louis J. Luzbetak, *The Church and Cultures* (Maryknoll, New York: Orbis, 1996), pp. 69-84. This work contains a helpful introductory section on contextualization.

the job, so to speak. Because people would look at the outside of our church and say that it was, you know, a picnic. But it has been really tough at times" (FG 90-93). In summary, the tough work of missional outreach proceeds as God uses flexible adapters in diverse contexts with a common vision of kingdom extension in church planting.

Fifth Subcategory: Self-Starter

Finally, a catalytic innovator is a self-starter. Without the traditional structures of church board and building — and with no traditions of worship style — the motivation of the new-church developer can lag. Added to this lack of structure is an informal (and perhaps impulsive) sense of decision-making and few or no people to implement the decisions (or just a small core group). In other words, the daily planning calendar can look painfully bare. The self-starter thrives in this empty landscape. The open calendar is a dream come true — or at least a dream in the making. It is the frequent fuel for action in effective leadership. Phillips says: "Leadership requires aggressive individuals — those who accept a 'take charge' role. Leaders, in general, are self-starting and change-oriented. They set a strategic direction and initiate as well as act. They achieve results as opposed to only carrying out activity."[18]

NCD pastors are sometimes keenly aware of the need for wide-open spaces of time and place in order to build. They know things happen when they make them happen. "One thing I would say is that the pastor-developer needs to be a self-starter. You need to be able to organize yourself, get up in the morning and do what you need to do, and then to help communicate some kind of vision to other people, so that they are ready to jump on board and feel like they can own it" (FG 94-96).

Of course, there are limits to how far one can drift in the real world. Even effective NCD pastors have financial responsibilities and, as a group, they are not independently wealthy. They have to work for a living. They have to pay the bills, and the need for financial stability can be a nagging pressure. To ease the burden, most of the church developers have seed-funding commitments for two to five years. Thus,

---

18. Phillips, *Lincoln on Leadership*, p. 108.

once they can stabilize the finances, they can move with zeal and directness. "We're going to do it [plant the church]," said one (FG 94-96). Once started, they did not look back. Another said: "If there is anything else in all creation that you can do, do it, but that's the negative way of saying you have got to be absolutely committed. Once you start this, you cannot stop" (FG 87-02).

Self-starters display real enthusiasm to press on. They act as spark plugs for ministries with reckless abandon. They move with tremendous "optimism in the sense that they just [don't] think about failure. They [believe] what they [are] about to do [is] going to succeed" (FG 87-89). A catalytic innovator has the ability to self-start the missional vision of the new congregation. He or she is not afraid to make decisions and opportunistically to carve out the right time to act, or, to put it another way, to make an action plan for ministry without traditional church support structures.

Taken as a whole, the catalytic innovator trait demonstrates that extraordinary new-church-development pastors are people on the move. They are not afraid to initiate a difficult plan of action or to take risks to see it through. They are creative innovators who see ways to persevere that others might miss, or might be unwilling to go the extra mile to realize. Above all else, they lead with charisma: they are gifted by God to be persons of influence. With this comes the necessity of maintaining a relationship with God. As a result, the next profile trait is of absolute importance.

Vibrant Faith in God

The second profile trait in the first tier is a "vibrant faith in God." Below are the responses from the most effective developers in their post-focus-group questionnaire:[19]

- Deep and sincere faith (2001-2002)
- Reliance on God (2001-2002)
- A deep faith in God (1987-1989)

---

19. Responses from all six post-focus-group surveys sorted by profile category "Vibrant Faith in God." For development of categories, see Merriam, p. 179.

- Faith (1987-1989)
- Passionate trust in God (1990-1993)
- Faith . . . a deep faith in God's calling, his provisions (1987-1989)
- Should know himself/herself and his/her faith (1994-1996)
- Need a positive understanding of one's own faith journey and spiritual commitment — and willing to share that with others (1994-1996)
- Clarity of call (1994-1996)
- Sense of call and personal faith relationship (1994-1996)
- Sense of call (1994-1996)
- Being intentional [about] Sabbath (2001-2002)
- Having an intentional prayer and devotional life (2001-2002)
- Study/spiritual discipline (1997-2000)
- Building an ongoing close and intimate relationship with God — to find joy and to hold you in tough times (1997-2000)
- Personal spiritual life and devotion (1997-2000)
- Bathe everything in prayer (1997-2000)
- Not take self too seriously; patience in prayer (1997-2000)
- "Letting God play through" and believing that it is his church (1997-2000)
- You can't give away what you don't have (1997-2000)
- Fill yourself up spiritually so you can spill over into the lives of others (1997-2000)
- A clear sense of what is; counting on God's Word and its importance; a clear statement of belief (1987-1989)
- Living, growing, vital relationship with Jesus Christ and a love for the Word (1987-1989)
- Has the passion and desire to abide in the presence of the head of the church; wants to know the Lord (1987-1989)
- Intimacy with God (1987-1989)
- Pray hard (1990-1993)
- Pray (1987-1989)
- Deep walk with God (1994-1996)
- Deep faith in God and oneself (1987-2002)
- Call/faith (1987-2002)
- Love of Christ; love of call (1987-2002)
- Christ-centered; spiritually rooted (1987-2002)
- Spiritual maturity and seasoned gifts for ministry (1987-2002)

• Prayer support and strong prayer life (1987-2002)
• Time for renewal (1987-2002)

Vibrant faith in God, as these developers attest, is rooted in "faith in God's calling, his provisions" (87-89). However, this is not a call to life in a spiritual comfort zone. These developers consistently need the close comfort of God, and they know that "you can't give away what you don't have" (97-00). Their lives are centered in "prayer support and [a] strong prayer life" (87-02). Vibrant means "pulsating with energy or activity"; "vibrant faith" describes a faith that abides, that is deep and active. Since Christian faith is a gift from God (Gal. 2:8-9), this trait indicates a continual journey of faith that is authentic and mature. In short, the NCD pastor is a person "allowing God to be God . . . believing that it is his church" (97-00).

> One of the pieces that keeps coming back to me in terms of a key word is "authenticity" when it comes to walking the faith. People want to know you're doing it. People want to know you love God. . . . [Jesus] needed to be fed by his Father. Lord knows we do. You know, [Jesus is] healing all these people, and they bring the next batch in and they can't find him. He's out on the hillside praying. If we, [if] any pastor, any faithful disciple, doesn't have some sort of discipline, prayer, meditation life, [we are] going to be empty before [we] know it. (FG 97-00; FG 01-02)

Vibrant faith in God is a trait to be nurtured, one that is cultivated and nourished by making prayer and reflection on Scripture a disciplined priority in life. This trait is quite unlike the action-oriented, hard-driving characteristics of the catalytic innovator, who seems to make things happen by sheer force of personality. Nonetheless, to be effective in new-church development, one must cultivate a vibrant faith rooted in Scripture. One developer describes this phenomenon as follows: "I think that pastors, entrepreneurs such as ourselves, we're driven by a lot of zeal, but that zeal needs to be based on knowledge. Romans 10 talks about that — and the feeding towards that knowledge — that comes from a personal, disciplined study of God's word, not just for the purpose of teaching it but for the enjoyment of it" (FG 94-96). Enjoyment of God is coupled with discernment through prayer. Some advice given by an effective developer underscores this point: "I would tell mission planters that first they need to have a prayer life. That's essential. Be aware of your own purpose as you seek God's purpose and a process for carrying God's purpose out" (FG 01-02).

This Christ-centered focus is energized in prayer. The contemplative exercise of prayer balances the energy of the self-starting charismatic leader. Taken together, these traits describe an active leader centered in contemplative prayer, which suggests that effective leadership is not rooted in personal strengths or mental acumen but in a strong and consistent walk with God. The following candid excerpts from church developers echo this theme well:

> If we don't have a prayer life, if we aren't taking daily time with God, then we get so filled with ourselves, there is no room left for the Spirit. Part of prayer, for me anyway, is very confessional, and it's very humbling in that sense. And, you know, that keeps me definitely very grounded and empty. [I] let God work through that. It gets to the fundamental question, you know, Who is going to lead this thing? Look at your track record and look at God's. Who do you want to be developing this mission? (FG 01-02)

> But at some point we have to rely on God and our gut, which is our heart, and let the Spirit guide us through it. (FG 01-02)

> I think the calling and the depth of personal spirituality go together, spiritual disciplines that people know . . . who you are in God. People around you know that you are the genuine deal, that you have been touched at the core of your being by God. And to me, that's number one, because . . . I've seen a whole lot of entrepreneurial stuff, and I've seen a lot of crashing and burning from entrepreneurial folks as well, those who don't have this part to balance it. (FG 94-96)

These leaders recognize that real church growth is a work of the Spirit. The prayer life of a congregation starts with the leader's life of prayer. Walking the talk of spirituality is acknowledged as being integral to the power behind the leadership. Jesus urged the first new-church developers to wait until they had received the power of the Spirit for faithful witness (Acts 1:8; 2:14-21). What these current developers practiced in their personal journeys of faith was extended as they sought prayer partnerships. One developer recounts: "We also had a hundred prayer partners. We sought out and got prayer support right away. That was a huge support in knowing you are connected and not out there — and connected to the larger group that is helping to make a difference" (FG 87-02). In his writings on leadership vision, Galloway emphasizes this same point:

> It is utterly impossible for you to expect your church to grow with-out prayer. Many mistakenly think that somehow if they get the right program then church growth will be automatic. This is a wrong approach. The moving power behind a growing church is fervent prayer. Early on in the book of Acts we see that signs and wonders and the church exploding in growth were a result of prayer . . . therefore, as church leaders we must make prayer a priority in our personal life and model prayer for our congregations.[20]

These leaders experienced the Spirit's movement as postmodern "sent-out" ones. They found the energy of the Spirit in their prayers.

Visionary/Vision Caster

The third profile trait of the first tier is that of a visionary/vision caster, a term that represents the third-most-cited leadership characteristic needed for an effective NCD pastor. Below are the comments of these leaders:[21]

- Ability to see the wider vision (2001-2002)
- Visioning capacity (2001-2002)
- Clarity of vision or purpose (1997-2000)
- Vision (1997-2000)
- A visionary (1987-1989)
- Have a vision of where the church is going (1987-1989)

20. Dale Galloway, *20/20 Vision: How to Create a Successful Church with Lay Pastors and Cell Groups* (Portland: Scott Publishing, 1986), p. 101.

21. Responses from all six post-focus-group surveys sorted by profile category "Visionary/Vision Caster." For development of categories, see Merriam, p. 179.

- Vision-renewal, re-evaluated every few years (1987-1989)
- Vision (1987-1989)
- Visionary/motivator (1987-1989)
- Have a big vision (1987-1989)
- Should have a good vision of the environment, the people, the community, the denomination, expectations, and resources (1994-1996)
- Clarity of vision (1994-1996)
- Visionary (1994-1996)
- Ability to relate and communicate vision to people (2001-2002)
- Vision-casting (2001-2002)
- Casting vision is the critical-continual task (1997-2000)
- Ability to form and convey a vision and core values (1997-2000)
- Vision development/-casting (1997-2000)
- Vision-casting ability (1997-2000)
- Vision-caster (1997-2000)
- Vision-casting (1990-1993)
- Share your vision with the body that God sends your way, and show members how they can be a part of it (1990-1993)
- Passion with a vision (articulated) (1990-1993)
- Holds out a vision and can articulate it (1990-1993)
- Articulate the vision of the church (1990-1993)
- Articulating a heartfelt passion/vision (1990-1993)
- Ability to motivate and inspire others (1994-1996)
- Visionary (1987-2002)
- Vision (1987-2002)
- Vision and focus (1987-2002)
- Clear vision (1987-2002)
- Creativity in vision (1987-2002)
- Absolute commitment to the importance of an engaging, transformative faith community (1987-2002)

These developers dreamed big dreams (87-89) and moved forward to fulfill them. They rooted these dreams in their understanding of God's purposes for the new church. They identified "casting vision as a critical-continual task" (97-00); they shared their "visioning capacity" (87-02, 01-02) with "the body that God sent" their way (90-93). They demonstrated an ability to "motivate and inspire" this body of new believers (94-96).

Survey results from the NCD leaders with the largest memberships reveal a higher degree of start-up focus on "reaching those not active in a church."[22] More importantly, these same top-membership-growth pastors were catalysts for creating a shared vision with their lay leaders, many of whom "shared the same vision for the church's future" and "received practical training for their respective responsibilities."[23] Most significantly, the NCD pastors with the largest memberships made "clearly articulating a vision for the congregation" a "very high priority" in their respective ministries.[24] However, the data from more than 700 NCD pastors — representing a greater than twenty-year span of ministry — are clear: NCD pastors experience huge gaps in the styles of their vision-casting. The most effective NCD pastors were more likely to cast "goals and objectives" statements as vision than to use the language of ideals and hopes that are found in traditional "vision statements." These leaders preferred to list the steps toward building the church — and they simply called these steps vision. This penchant, incidentally, distinguishes these leaders from their smaller-membership colleagues, for whom this kind of vision-casting was a lesser priority.[25]

The top developers cast a working vision with clarity, and they manifested the kind of leadership that Phillips speaks of: "The first dictionary definition of a 'leader' describes a primary shoot of a plant, the main artery through which the organism lives and thrives. In much the same way,

22. Survey Q-31a findings: Pastors of 541+ membership churches and 305+ membership churches rated between 8 percent and 15 percent higher than did smaller-membership church pastors in their exacting vision to focus their NCD ministry during the first two years after the first public worship on "reaching those not active in a church."

23. Survey Q-31b findings: Pastors of 541+ membership churches rated between 22 percent and 29 percent higher than did smaller-membership church pastors in effectively establishing church leaders who "shared the same vision for the church's future," and they were 20 percent more likely to have received "practical training for their respective responsibilities" (Q-31c) than were the NCD leaders with 100 members or fewer.

24. Survey Q-40d findings: Pastors of 541+ membership churches and 305+ memberships rated between 24 percent and 25 percent higher than smaller-membership church pastors in "clearly articulating a vision for the congregation" as a "very high priority."

25. Survey Q-40e findings: Pastors of 541+ membership churches rated 29 percent higher than did smaller-membership church pastors with 100 or fewer members in "developing goals and objectives" as a "very high priority" in "providing leadership" for their new church start.

organizations prosper or die as a result of the leader's ability to embody and communicate the company's vision."[26] Vision-focused and mission-driven is what sums up these leaders. They believe that God is up to something in their ministries, and they pursue their vision of God's purpose relentlessly. Their energetic and imaginative leading vision, coupled with their vibrant faith, fuels the Spirit's. They spoke of vision this way:

> I found that consensus will kill you. It will absolutely kill a new church. [You have to say:] Here's where we're going. Blow the trumpet. Sound the horn. Let's go. If you want to get on the train, fine. If you don't, go find another train to hop. [We can't survive with] "let's just talk about it." (FG 90-93)

> [One must have a] very, very clear sense of vision. Such a clear sense of vision that, during the first couple of years, when you have so many other demands on your time, so many new people coming in with so many different requests and needs . . . [those demands] can't stretch you away. [The ministry itself] can divert you away from the vision and the mission of the church. And so I think that's one real key emphasis for a founding pastor or missionary pastor of a new church — vision. (FG 94-96)

> The people from this new congregation need to have a clear, strong sense of conviction that this is a God thing, that the church isn't going to shoot it down or save it because it's growing, but that God has had his hand in this and called me and there's work to do here. So the expectation is that God is going to do something here. (FG 87-89)

> The vision comes from the Spirit, and we help shape that in terms of helping those folks who are gathered to see it within themselves and to see it together and to be creative in the way that we imagine the future together, in how we move and how we grow. (FG 87-02)

Not everyone in the membership of the NCD catches the vision. Those who do "get it" form the membership focus of these new congregations. Discipleship and membership are tied to the vision. Hence,

---

26. Phillips, *Lincoln on Leadership*, p. 162.

membership involves "infecting" the new church with the spiritual DNA of the vision. It involves getting on board with the new church's vision. Casting the vision and helping new members catch the vision go hand in hand.

In his book *First Things First,* Stephen Covey speaks of vision and vision-casting as the clock and the compass:

> Our struggle to put first things first can be characterized by the contrast between two powerful tools that direct us: the clock and the compass. The clock represents our commitments, appointments, schedule, goals activities — what we do with and how we manage our time. The compass represents our vision, values, principles, mission, conscience, direction — what we feel is important and how we lead our lives. The struggle comes when we sense a gap between the clock and the compass. . . .[27]

To produce a successful NCD, the clock and the compass must be aligned. Shared vision in the grand plan must link to membership in the new church. This relational implementation and the ability to pull it off are integral to being an effective vision-caster. The top new-church developers describe the alignment of vision and membership as follows:

> I think the vision is a very important thing. If you don't know where you're going, people are going to know that. You have got to know where you're going. . . . We made a decision early on that we were not going to be a membership congregation, we were going to be a discipleship congregation. So I've never focused on membership, even though obviously from the bureaucratic end of the church, you've got to have the statistical data. But we have focused on making disciples and covenanting to be disciples. We have the marks of discipleship and that has made a huge difference. I think it's brought people deeper into the workings of the ministry of the church rather than thinking, "I can come in, sign this piece of paper, I'm a member, and now I can sit back and relax." It's not a health club, where you pay your dues and come whenever you feel like it. We're looking for partners, not members. (FG 01-02)

27. Stephen Covey, *First Things First* (New York: Free Press, 1996), pp. 19-20.

We have a new member class, and much of that class is really saying to people, "This is our vision, and if you don't like it, there [are] probably in our area 500 other churches and, you know, you would be welcome at any of those, but this is what we're doing. So please get on board with it, and if you're not on board, you can come all you want, but don't try to change it, because this is it." (FG 01-02)

I think what we ended up with, and why the others have failed, is that they used a shotgun approach and tried to hit everybody's buttons. We did not do that. (FG 97-00)

In our class, we cast a vision of what it means to live a passion for God and try to bring people in, walk them through that whole vision. At the end of it, we're very blunt about what we expect from members. We have a membership commitment form. When they come forward on the day they join, they sign the membership commitment form. This past year, we've ramped it up so we're now saying to people, "If you desire to be a member of [our church], members have to do ministry. If you don't want to do ministry, that's fine, we love having you around, hang around all you want to, be a part of this place — but you can't be a member, because members do ministry." (FG 97-00)

These vision-casters build communities of faith that share their vision. They manage to get things done without succumbing to the role of manager and neglecting visionary leadership. Relying on the Spirit, they continually draw a new community of people into the church, and incoming new members catch the vision the innovative leader casts. Their leadership is not muddied by "clock" necessities of moment; instead, they are energized to pull their emerging congregations toward the emerging mission of the church. Of course, these leaders are not creating cults; they do not command the vision. They inspire. They lead. They motivate. Within their inspirational and enthusiastic leadership we see the true etymology of the word *enthusiastic,* meaning "God-inspired."

Conclusion

The purpose of this chapter has been to "unpack" in some detail the Tier 1 characteristics that effective NCD pastors consider crucial to their success. There are three characteristics of effective church developers: 1) catalytic innovator; 2) vibrant faith in God; and 3) visionary/vision-caster. Taken together, these three represent almost half (48 percent) of all comments explaining success. It is important to remember that these characteristics are derived from the analysis of focus-group discussions; they are neither psychometric measures nor behavioral indices. For that reason, their power and ability to inform is both limited and focused. These factors can tell us relatively little about what is conclusively "true" about effective new-church development. They can, however, give us quite powerful indications about what those who are doing new-church development effectively consider to be conclusively true. From their insights we may draw the following conclusions. First, those involved in developing and expanding churches may need to cultivate a new slate of competencies for selecting leaders. The leaders most effective in developing new churches are not conformists but catalysts. They are not marginal believers; they cultivate vibrant faith. They are not half-hearted achievers; they cast bold and risky visions, and they expect to be followed. This constellation of traits can run counter to the popular notions of leaders as "team players" or even "servant leaders." These are leaders tremendously invested in people, but they are also zealously and unwaveringly invested in a vision. The paradigm for missional growth may involve inviting an aggressive, action-oriented bull into the china shop of church tradition.

Of course, these leaders do not lead in a vacuum. They have followers who make the vision manifest. This is, as this chapter suggests, not a smooth and easy process. Even in the best of circumstances, leading new congregations is hard work. New churches have soaring peaks and perilous chasms. These leaders have a keen understanding of self, of God's call, and of a vision of the Kingdom of God in particular ministry contexts. Despite external challenges and the spiritual challenges of affirming the Christian faith, they press on unreservedly in God's call to plant a community of faithful witnesses.

It is important to remember that the success of these effective developers must be juxtaposed against a landscape of tremendous loss.

Each of the seven denominations stipulated in this study is losing more members each year than it is gaining. Each denomination admits to having many established congregations in need of transformational leadership and redevelopment. Developing new churches is seen as one of the hopes for the future for these denominations. Nonetheless, many of the new churches planted by these denominations have produced only marginal results.[28] This study suggests that a very specialized set of personality traits and behavioral characteristics may be necessary to new-church growth. Training and placing clergy who lack these foundational traits may produce only a mediocre harvest at best.

The qualitative research of this study has identified a unique group of profile traits that seem inherent to effectiveness. If this can be taken to mean that church and lay leaders should be actively nurturing and calling such leaders, then a compelling question arises: What percentage of existing ordained clergy, or those in training for ordination, might display these characteristics? Given the losses that continue to be sustained among these seven denominations, the number must be painfully small — or the barriers to unleash these leaders particularly cumbersome.

This chapter suggests characteristics that form the hallmarks of leadership. If these effective NCD leaders — and others like them — are to be welcomed into positions of pivotal leadership, denominations and training institutions will have to be receptive to them. The solution to the staggering losses experienced by these seven denominations is not to be found in business as usual. It is not a remedy found in more judicatory planning, or new-church-growth programming, or even in a disembodied theory of applied evangelical theology. This chapter suggests that leaders who are trained to exercise these gifts responsibly and maturely will thrive in new-church development. Those interested in future missional growth would benefit by nurturing those who display this combination of learned skills and special charisma.

Second, all of these effective NCD pastors successfully navigated through the educational and ordination requirements typical of

28. For example, in the Presbyterian Church (USA) in a ten-year period of new-church development during the study period, a high percentage of the hoped-for larger-membership new churches stopped growing at fewer than 150 in worship. All of these new congregations were started in high-growth residential areas.

Protestant denominations in twenty-first-century America. With few variations, clergy in these denominations matriculate through undergraduate school, complete seminary training on the graduate level, and pass ordination examinations. Given the intensity, duration, and regimentation of these demands, it is amazing that leaders who possess these traits ever clear the hurdles. The fact that catalytic innovators can even run the gauntlet of denominational call is surprising. Perhaps most surprising is that the gauntlet is geared to producing ministers for existing churches, not new churches. Many of the skills found in catalytic innovators, such as leadership, perseverance, risk-taking, adapting, and the organizational aspects of self-starting, are learnable skills. Granted, some of these traits are raw charisma and as such are God-given; and as such they can be either sublimated or cultivated.

This chapter touches the boundary of further research and further reflection. Embedded in future research is a surprising question: How might this study inform seminary education, field experience, and professional recruitment? What would these training and placement venues look like if qualifying for leadership meant showing the potential for building an evangelizing community of faith where large portions of the congregants were formerly unchurched? Placement in a ministry setting where ministry skills taught in classrooms can be practiced in faith communities is not a new paradigm for theological education. Some form of this paradigm exists in the requirements for certain core courses of seminary curricula, seminary field education, and clinical pastoral education. The results discussed in this chapter force us to ask whether this combination of critical profile traits is being taught in denominational seminaries or caught in supervised ministry assignments. In a church atmosphere where charismatic leadership might be rightfully questioned, might it also be valued as a gift of the Holy Spirit and nurtured by classroom learning and practice? This chapter raises questions about the appropriateness of our paradigms for leadership preparation.

Third, since the training places where missional church vision can be caught and taught are relatively few, it is possible that traditional denominations can learn from experimental training used increasingly by nondenominational churches. Unencumbered by the bureaucratic processes that are attached to traditional Protestant clergy preparation, many large nondenominational churches have become, in effect, mini-seminaries. These churches select, nurture, and train evangelizing witnesses, then mentor them closely. Those who participate find a home of like minds. This is, sadly, not true of many of the NCD pastors who participated in this study. Although not expressly discussed in this chapter, one strong inference to be drawn from the views of these NCD pastors is that they form a distinctive breed. Despite denominational differences, many of these pastors had much more in common with each other than with the traditional pastors from their respective denominations back home. This chapter, then, raises questions about the formation of supportive faith communities for these pastors, both within the seminary and beyond.

In the next chapter we describe the second tier of NCD pastors' traits. These traits include the ability to empower the people around them, attending to personal and relational health, and focusing on worship and preaching. Although these are ranked lower than the top tier by these pastors, these form a powerful balance to the traits discussed in this chapter. If the top-tier traits can be characterized as the spark plugs, then the second-tier traits form the fuel. Without both, the car may be dazzling and new, but it will not run. Both are necessary, dependent, intertwined. Placing this next set of traits into "Tier 2" implies no lessening of importance in the minds of these pastors; rather, it may simply suggest that these pastors felt that no one would attempt to run a car without fuel. It is to this second tier that we now turn.

Chapter Three

The Tier-Two
Characteristics of an Effective
New-Church-Development Pastor

H. STANLEY WOOD

Introduction

The ability to see and create a new church where none existed before seems to require the spiritual gifts and learned skills of the catalytic innovator, the one with a vibrant faith in God, and the visionary/visioncaster. These could be considered the spark plugs of the NCD engine. It is possible to have the outward body of a car (the denominational and administrative structure) and the fuel (traits we will examine in this chapter); but without the spark plugs to ignite the engine, the NCD is likely to sputter. Hence, the top tier of traits seems crucial to both immediate and long-term success. However, an NCD pastor with a bold flair, a risky vision, and a flamboyant missionary zeal probably will not succeed without a mature and reasonable understanding of when and how to invite discipline and structure into the mix. Thus the second tier of traits, which might be described as more administrative and bureaucratic in nature, is as crucial to success as the first tier. Although they are more bureaucratic, these traits are imbued with the subtle energy of timing, with the delicate balance of individual personalities and collective energy, and with the process of yielding to a corporate vision that is expressed in a wider circle of believers.

The second tier of leadership traits provides further insights into how these top developers identify the skills that are necessary to grow the NCD from individual vision to community life. Again, these gifts are distinguishable from the top tier only in numerical rank. They constitute a separate, but no less critical, mix of gifts; and it would be inappropriate to divorce them from the top tier of gifts. In fact, the categories of the second tier are intimately interconnected with the first tier in the missional task of new-church development. Without this interlink, a new-church development would jerk and sputter to a halt.

It is important to say at the outset that most of the traits listed here can be found in catalog listings of "spiritual gifts" in the New Testament. Some might suggest that, if such traits are, in fact, spiritual gifts, then it might be useless for seminaries, churches, or denominational governing bodies to pay attention to such things as education, training, and practice. Some might assume that those to whom the gifts are given will find outlets and means to exercise their gifts, no matter what. Some might further suppose that persons with these gifts will succeed under any conditions, while those without the gifts will fail no matter what. There are difficulties embedded in this posture, so a further explication of the understanding of the relationship between spiritual gifts and learnable skills is in order.

We are told that there are those to whom spiritual gifts are given by God, that these gifts may include, for example, preaching or evangelism. However, history teaches us that not all preachers or evangelists in the church have had these gifts — or they have not honed their gifts. Assume for the moment that three categories of people are aspiring to ordination: 1) those who have been gifted by God as preachers or evangelists; 2) those who do not have the gifts initially but who, over time, are given them by God; and 3) those who are not gifted in these ways but nonetheless feel called to ministry. What seminaries can (and should) offer these three groups of candidates is education, training, practice, and time. Those in the first category, it may be assumed, will advance beyond their peers. However, those in the second and third groups can acquire competence in these areas, and they may, over time, become exceptional in them.

It is of greatest importance for us to understand that preachers and evangelists are, in the end, quite like opera singers and surgeons. They may be born with the gift, but unless they subject that gift to discipline and education, it can atrophy. It can even die. Therefore, though these traits may be cited from time to time as gifts, it is implicitly understood that these gifts necessarily require education, training, practice, and time to make them useful. Throughout this chapter, then, we emphasize the acquisition of skills. This is not to downplay the importance or grace of a God-given spiritual gift; it is merely to underscore the vital importance of the discipline required to hone that gift into something synergistic in ministry.

The second tier is composed of the following categories:

Tier 2	Empowering leadership	8%
	Passion for people	7%
	Personal and relational health	7%
	Passion for faith-sharing	7%
	Inspiring preaching and worship	7%
		36%

Note that the percentage ranks among these five traits are almost uniformly equal. Therefore, it is statistically impossible to create a hierarchical distinction among these traits. In a sense, they can be viewed as one interconnected gift with equally weighted subcategories. For our purposes, we will view them as a block of traits, each carrying equal weight and significance.[1]

Empowering Leadership

Here are the top developer responses gathered in the first category of Tier Two, empowering leadership:[2]

- Experiencing leading/empowering/delegating others (2001-2002)
- Identify and train leaders who understand the mission and vision of the congregation (2001-2002)

---

1. The percentage difference between them is 1 percent; thus they need to be viewed as a group of profile categories, each of which is equally significant. Indeed, these are complementary to the profile traits found in Tier One, and they are sometimes integral to effective behavior.

2. Responses from all six post-focus-group surveys sorted by profile category "empowering leadership." For development of categories, see Sharon B. Merriam, "Constant Comparative Method," in *Qualitative Research and Case Study Applications in Education*, 2nd ed. (San Francisco: Jossey-Bass, 1998), p. 179.

- Willingness to give up ministry to gifted lay people (2001-2002)
- Team building/leadership sharing (can be successful at the onset without this) (1997-2000)
- Recruiting ability (1997-2000)
- Team deployment ability (1997-2000)
- Realizing the gifts of each person; God will bring all the gifts necessary to build his church (1997-2000)
- Team builder/equipper (1987-1989)
- Delegating (1987-1989)
- Giving ministry to the lay people (1987-1989)
- Cooperating/willing to accept guidance; partnership with others (1994-1996)
- Leadership development (2001-2002)
- Leadership (1997-2000)
- Leadership training (1997-2000)
- Developing a group of leaders who will share the ministry passion (1990-1993)
- Giving ministry away to those leaders (1990-1993)
- Ability to spot leaders (1994-1996)
- Ability to train laity (or get them to training) (1987-2002)
- Delegating (1987-2002)
- Being willing to mentor (1987-2002)
- Engaging lay people from the very beginning; allowing people to have ownership in the process (1987-2002)

Empowering leadership does not mean, as the popular phrase has it, merely "working smart." This brand of leadership is not simply energetic leading; it is also the "ability to spot" and nurture other leaders (FG 94-96). Maxwell puts it this way: "There is something more scarce than [recruitment] ability: it is the ability to recognize the ability. One of the primary responsibilities of successful leaders is to identify potential leaders."[3] Highly effective NCD developers put a continuous and urgent premium on the identification and training of indigenous leadership. As a result, these leaders are probably the least likely to rely on judicatory staff or national denominational staff to do their lay

3. John Maxwell, *Developing the Leader Within You* (Nashville: Thomas Nelson, 1995), p. 37.

training.[4] Although these pastors tend to trust their own ability to spot and train leaders, they do not shoulder the whole burden for leadership development. They are, for example, more likely than smaller-membership NCD leaders to seek personal leadership training from seminary faculty.[5]

What is perhaps most fascinating about the leadership styles of these extraordinary developers is that they have not had more experience in leading or in training leaders than have their less successful NCD colleagues.[6] However, these top developers place leadership training near the top of their list of priorities, and they devote their time and energies to it.[7] In fact, their investment of time and the training of specific tasks within the growing ministry are strategically focused. For instance, the top developers report that their members are more likely to receive practical training in a broad range of membership responsibilities. Once they have trained these lay leaders, developers use them as a key source for contacting unchurched prospects, as well as sponsoring formerly unchurched persons as they enter the community of faith.[8]

Below are some verbal snapshots of how the top developers described their leadership training, recruitment, and delegation:

4. The quantitative survey Q-14c indicates that lay leader training in the largest NCDs (over 400+ in attendance and more than 541+ members) used judicatory staff 10 percent to 14 percent less than all other NCD pastors surveyed; according to the survey Q-15c responses, the top developers used national denominational staff 0 percent, compared to some medium-size NCDs (with 126 to 225 in worship) who used national staff 22 percent of the time for lay training.

5. Quantitative survey Q-16d showed that smaller-membership NCD pastors did this 3 percent to 6 percent of the time, versus larger-membership pastors, who sought help for NCD leadership 14 percent of the time during the first two years after public worship was held.

6. In survey Q-22b, the top developers scored only a negligible 3 percent to 4 percent over the next two highest NCD membership sizes in their experience and training of laypersons.

7. In survey Q-30d, the top developers scored 10 percent higher than all other NCD pastors in placing "a great deal" of time on lay training.

8. Survey Q-31c indicates that lay leaders in top developers' congregations were 7 percent to 30 percent more likely to receive practical training in their respective responsibilities, as well as to be used as a major source for contacting unchurched prospects (Q-31e), and approximately 30 percent more likely to mentor or sponsor the unchurched contacts in church membership.

Training

I think it's training and training and training and training and training. Because they [new lay leaders] may move away with all the training you are giving them. So you are training and training and training new flocks all the time. Then [you begin] delegating and having some healthy people you hire into those roles. . .[people] who are really competent and can carry it off. [You begin] getting all those variables to work together to take it to that next level. . . . I am powered by the energy and ingenuity of the developer, but all those [lay leaders] have to come together to bump it up to the next level. (FG 87-02)

Recruitment

I can remember when someone challenged me to punch the word "pastor" into my computer and "Bible" and see what came up. [That's when] I took the sign "Senior Pastor" off my door and put "Equipment Room" on the door, and just said, "We're going to equip people to do ministry." (FG 97-00)

Delegation

You are the magnet and you do attract [people]. At the same time you have to know it's not you, that it is God's work that is happening. [You have to know that] your job is not only the magnet. You also are trying to help the people understand that they have to go beyond you in order to become the church and grow the ministry. People [can then] begin to see how they can function together in ministry. (FG 87-89)

You get individual members involved in ministries [who are] touching the needs of the people in the community. You turn people loose. It's that "priesthood of all believers" concept that's been around. You turn them loose in ministries, and you give them permission to care. You don't put them on a board. You don't put them on a committee. You don't make ushers out of them. You make ministers out of them and put them in situations where they're dealing with life issues of normal human beings. And that draws. (FG 87-89)

We decided we'll only have ministry teams and they'll be commissioned to do their work without getting approval. We write a job description for each ministry team, [give them the] parameters, give them X number of dollars and say, "Go do it." They have an elder coach. The elder coach is to make sure that they inspire and communicate to the session, et cetera. But the elders do very little administrative work. The teams are commissioned and empowered and given authority to do their work without getting our approval, which makes things happen a lot faster. It requires an enormous amount of trust between the elders and the team leaders. It frees them up and it says, "We trust you. You believe in what we're trying to do here. Now go do it." (FG 01-02)

In essence, the core behavior of these top developers is that they lead to give their leadership away. However, they don't give authority away carelessly or haphazardly. They are willing to take the lead, but they are also willing to give the lead away to those who have been trained to step into authority. This is a very old and, to many in the church, recognizable model of leadership and leadership training. It is, of course, the way Jesus trained his disciples to take the responsibility for creating the very first new-church development. These top developers do not fill their leadership roles as seamlessly or perfectly as Jesus did, but they recognize that they could stall the Spirit's work and create administrative bottlenecks by holding on to the lead. However imperfectly they may engage in the process, these leaders make a priority of training and delegating leaders among the laity.

It is interesting that one of the developers quotes the seminal Reformed concept of the "priesthood of all believers" as a justification for the work of leadership training. It is an appropriate paradigm. Spotting leaders, nurturing the gifts of leadership, challenging and inspiring lay leaders to act on a shared vision is part of a long tradition in Christianity: it was seen in Christ, in the early church, in the Reformers, and in the many who are working to develop ministries worldwide. It is certainly proving to be a powerful model of leadership for top developers engaged in NCD ministries.

Passion for People

Here are the top developers' responses gathered into the second category of Tier Two: passion for people.[9]

- Passion! For the vision, and for people (2001-2002)
- Genuine love for people (2001-2002)
- Being "with" people at their point of need (2001-2002)
- Good relational and people skills (2001-2002)
- Compassion for all people; passionate about things Jesus was passionate about (1997-2000)
- Effective people skills (1987-1989)
- Able to work well with people of all ages (1987-1989)
- People skills — with a genuine deep faith in God (1987-1989)
- Relational (1994-1996)
- Makes a lot of contacts (1987-1989)
- Strong people skills (1990-1993)
- Relational (1990-1993)
- Demonstrates a spirit of warmth, friendliness, and acceptance of people (1990-1993)
- Open personality (good listener) (1994-1996)
- Should probably be an extrovert (1994-1996)
- Love of congregation and community context (1987-2002)
- Relates well with people (1987-2002)
- Welcoming personality (1987-2002)
- Love people where they are (1987-2002)

It is obvious that these leaders, who are energetic about tasks and structure, genuinely want to be centered in their relationships with others. Thus they can achieve a balance of priorities. These leaders love, they care, and they show it — and they identify relational skills as a key ingredient of leadership in the success of any new church. Interestingly, there is a symbiotic relationship between this "passion for people" trait and a trait discussed in the previous chapter — vision-caster. It would seem that lead-

9. The category "passion for people" is derived from 19 responses (or 7 percent) of the total post-focus-group questionnaire citations. Note that this is the same percent as the Tier Two profile points of "personal and relational health," "passion for faith-sharing," and "inspiring preaching and worship."

ers who succeed must combine, in equally zealous and authentic parts, the qualities of passion and vision. In short, leaders must first learn to speak the contextual language of the initial gathering congregation. Then they must possess the ability to establish meaningful dialogue between the needs, hopes, and dreams embedded within the existing community and translate these into the purpose of the new church. These are leaders whose passion is both internal and external. They not only feel for those to whom they minister, but they also can demonstrate their passion in appropriate and meaningful ways. They can connect with people.

Top developers can forge a unified ministry that is charged with both passion and vision. They skillfully connect with people and explore how the future of God's kingdom purposes might be realized in that relationship. It is significant that their leadership style is a dialogue, not a monologue. Reuel Howe, in his book *The Miracle of Dialogue,* describes dialogue as essential to building every strong and honest relationship: "Dialogue in a relationship is what blood is to the body. When the flow of blood stops, the body dies. When the flow of dialogue stops, the relationship dies."[10]

One NCD developer describes this dialogue as the heart of information gathering, evangelism, and vision-casting:

> One other thing that I did when I started: it was trying to get the pulse of people. I did some focus groups and met one-on-one with people who were not currently going to church. [I'd spend time] with three, four, five people. I asked everybody, "Do you know anybody that doesn't go to church?" I called [those people] up. They were pretty open to it. A couple of people said they wouldn't come. I met some people for coffee and just asked them, "Why don't you go to church? What might encourage you to go to church?" (FG 01-02)

Initiating a new church that specifically welcomes the outsider is important. The church developers build core relationships with those who have been outside the church. However, developing close relationships with the unchurched is not the only relational skill these leaders use. In addition, they spot leadership potential in the emerging congregation. Effective NCD leaders begin to develop and nurture relationships with these nascent leaders using the lifeblood of dialogue.

10. Reuel L. Howe, *The Miracle of Dialogue* (Greenwich, Conn.: Seabury, 1963), p. i.

These leaders also use these strategic relationships to multiply their contacts within their ministry context. The survey findings, from more than 700 NCD pastors and over a twenty-year period, indicate that, during the first year of worship, effective NCD pastors begin to function as "big church" pastors, even though their churches are still quite small. For example, in churches destined to be both rapidly growing and yet eventually stable in membership size, these effective pastors were less likely to spend time meeting with groups in the community than were smaller-membership NCD pastors. Instead, they express their passion for people by networking with emerging congregational leaders, thus augmenting their contacts with the unchurched. The top developers are "people persons" — but with a focus on each relationship. For example, survey results indicate that effective developers score higher than all other NCD pastors in establishing visitor follow-up programs, in placing a high priority on inspiring and motivating members to be involved in the community, and, most importantly, in prizing the skill of listening carefully to the needs of people.[11]

Here is that delicate and dynamic process described in their own words:

> The fact of the matter is, you don't have a building or a choir or an organ or a staff. There are all kinds of very prosperous churches around you, [at least] there were [several] where we were. [During] maybe the first six months, twelve months, eighteen months, you are the magnet that's sort of holding that thing together, at least for a while. And then it has to grow beyond that, [and you] just

---

11. In survey question Q-30c, the top developers spent 9 percent to 14 percent less time than all other NCD pastors meeting with groups in the community; in Q-31d, the top developers had up to 24 percent more points of contact in the local community than did other NCD pastors; Q-31c shows that the top developers demonstrated 10 percent to 29 percent more propensity to network with their membership as a major source for contacting unchurched persons; Q-31f indicated that when the unchurched person was tracked in relational follow-up, the top developers universally checked the highest categories, which indicated that they did follow-up quite "well," while other smaller-membership NCD pastors were less likely to do so — from 7 percent up to 40 percent of the time. Finally, in Q-39a, top developers scored 14 percent to 18 percent higher than all other NCD pastors in placing a very high priority on inspiring and motivating members' involvement in the community and 10 percent to 21 percent higher on listening to and responding to people's needs. Hence, the top developers indicated a strong passion for people.

[have] to be aware of that. Otherwise, if they don't have that contact with you, if they don't see you as their pastor and [as the] embodiment of the church — because there is no physical church — I mean, everything we had was in the trunk of my car. If that doesn't happen, you're in trouble. That's just, I think, essential to that process. Then later — I mean, hopefully people come to the church — and I don't want to oversimplify this, but the ministry of the church takes hold and they become involved and they appreciate all the good programs that you have.

Initially you don't have a lot of that programming, so there has to be a personal kind of [connection]. And later it's not, "Look where I am!" It's always completely different. A lot of our members, I'm not sure whether they know my name, [and my name is] not important. But they're a part of a community of faith, and their spiritual needs are being met from a whole smorgasbord of ministries you offer them. (FG 87-89)

Another [strategy for growth] was to get people together no matter how small the group was [to form] what I call a "critical mass." That was to begin to help them to relate to one another. So we had a lot of fellowship events just to have people kind of pick up on the enthusiasm of starting something new. And that is a fun kind of experience, I think, for lay people to think they're laying the foundation stones for an institution, an organization [that] is going to be around for a very, very long time to come. (FG 87-89)

Back then and [even] today I still have in the back of my mind always an atmosphere or climate of warmth and welcome of acceptance. I think that's what motivated me. And I think there have been surveys made that people are coming looking for friendships, and [the] most important friendship they first identify [in] a church is [with] the pastor — his [or her] openness, his [or her] warmth, his [or her] willingness to get to know them. [You have to] memorize their names, welcome them. [It's] remembering conversations, little things they express about their needs. (FG 90-93)

These leaders are eloquently describing a relationship-rich ministry. They contact people, they listen for the needs of their congregation, and they care for others with passion. Their ministries could be called "focused relational ministries." Kouzes and Posner describe a profile of leadership as an emotional contract between leaders and followers: "People must believe that leaders understand their needs and have their interests at heart."[12] This passion for people will welcome the outsider into the church fold. It is the kind of passion demonstrated by Jesus when he heard the woman at the well express her need for water. Jesus heard her, but he translated the need she expressed into her real need for spiritual nourishment in language she could grasp.[13] Jesus' actions speak about a focus of ministry on the lost, the outsider, coupled with a focus on spiritual needs.

The top church developers we profiled show some of the same focus when they describe their passion for people:

> I would add another level or aspect of communication, which is being relational with people. [It's] the kind of interaction where, in their story, their history, their reality, there is something that I can tap into and, as a new-church development pastor, understand. (FG 94-96)

> So a healthy church has that full orbit of ministry, but has very much a focused energy on the end product, which is what it means to be a disciple. (FG 01-02)

> I hear that a lot from people, you know, "You are real," when they first come as unchurched people. "I could relate to you. You weren't up there as an authority telling me what I should do. You were in there walking with [me]." (FG 01-02)

It seems obvious that these NCD pastors derive a portion of their energy and motivation from being with people.[14] However, this

12. James M. Kouzes and Barry M. Posner, *The Leadership Challenge* (San Francisco: Jossey-Bass, 1995), p. 11.

13. In the 4th chapter of the Gospel of John, Jesus crosses two first-century cultural boundaries: a man talking to a woman and a Jew talking to a Samaritan. He related to her at the level of physical thirst, which drew them both to the well, and then he offered to quench her real thirst: he offered her "living water," to be found in relationship to him as Messiah.

14. Survey Q-36g indicated that most top developers were more likely to be extro-

does not necessarily suggest that extroverts make better — or more effective — NCD pastors than introverts do. Indeed, this is not the case. A passion for people is a learned skill, not an inherent personality characteristic; it refers to the skill or the spiritual gift of building spiritual relationships using pastoral skills (Eph. 4:10-18). This unique kind of NCD leadership ignites a flame of enthusiasm for others while kindling a compelling vision for God's calling and the sending of the church in mission. This demanding skill does not call the pastor to dismiss or ignore the rest of life in service to the church. Instead, the most effective NCD pastors learn to balance the exciting call of mission with the quieter, but no less important, call of becoming mature human beings. Attending to personal self-care and relationships with family and friends requires a balancing act. To do it, these effective NCD pastors learn to practice the boundaries we discuss in our next profile trait.

Personal and Relational Health

Here are the top developers' responses gathered into the third category of Tier Two: personal and relational health.[15]

---

verts — that is, they received "energy by being with people" — than introverts, whose energy is usually depleted by people ministry. But it should be noted that a significant minority of these top developers (15 percent) did not indicate a propensity for being energized by being with people. Therefore, we did not list extroversion as a profile trait, since survey Q-36g also identified top developers who disagreed with the notion of being energized by being with people. Q-36g shows that a significant minority of top developers demonstrated introvert propensities. What does this mean? It seems that the key to a passion for people is not based on being an extrovert or an introvert. The behavior evidenced in "passion for people" can be embodied more effortlessly by extroverts; however, since a "passion for people" is seen in a significant number of top developers who register introverted tendencies, we may assume that these top developers demonstrate counter-intuitive people skills and thus function in NCD leadership as gregarious and highly socialized people. Anecdotally, it is interesting to note that most of the 15 percent were all top NCD developers in the Presbyterian Church (USA).

15. Responses from post-focus-group questionnaires of top developers: 18 responses (equaling 7 percent) of the total citations (same percent as Tier Two profile points of "passion for people," "passion for faith-sharing," and "inspiring preaching and worship"). Unlike all the profile points before or after this one, the inclusion of "personal and relational health" as a profile point in Tier Two is because of the strong

- Be honest in your self-assessment. Has God given you the gifts to do this? (1990-1993)
- Sense of self that is apart from one's work (1987-2002)
- Good boundaries (1987-2002)
- Emotional stability (1987-2002)
- Secure with God and family (2001-2002)
- Spousal cooperation (2001-2002)
- Family support system (2001-2002)
- Building a strong family life (1997-2000)
- Good health — a supportive spouse [if married] (1987-1989)
- Critical to take care of self and family and to find some support/ sharing group to be a part of (1994-1996)
- Solid spiritual life — daily devotional times; healthy, supportive marriage (1994-1996)
- Commitment to Jesus Christ as Savior and Lord and desire to role model that in 1) own life, 2) marriage, 3) family, and 4) community (1997-2000)
- Energy (1990-1993)
- Energy (1987-1989)
- Energy (1987-2002)
- Lots of energy (1987-2002)
- High energy (1987-2002)

Personal and relational health explicitly identifies healthy self-love in keeping body, mind, and spirit aligned and healthy. Most importantly, this trait underscores the importance of attending to and nurturing healthy families. Most of the top church developers are married.[16] The demands of NCD work, particularly in the initiating years, can put significant strains on family relationships. Keeping a marriage strong and families thriving requires a disciplined adherence to boundaries and a commitment to deepening relationships. Though this is absolutely necessary, it is not easy. The balancing of disparate commitments requires sacrifice, a sense of priorities, and the willingness to

---

emphasis of women NCD pastors on relational health in the family and relational care for children in particular.

16. Survey Q-48 indicates that 93 percent were married; of those interviewed in focus groups, the few who were not married do not compose a large enough number to be statistically significant.

choose the most important matters in life from among a competitive and demanding field of good things. This is the struggle, according to the following comments from top developers:

> So there were some sacrifices. Our kids still talk about it and laugh about it, say how much fun that was. Nobody remembers what he or she got for Christmas in '87 or '89, but everybody remembers the cars we drove and the piles of people in the house for Bible studies and meetings. (FG 90-93)

> New mission developers who are married — [whether you are a woman or a man] — you've got to work that stuff out with your [spouse] that you're making a sacrifice here. These people are going to be in your house. You can't walk around in your underwear anymore. (FG 90-93)

Laughing about sacrifices is often easier to do in hindsight than it is in the face of lifestyle changes that new-church start-ups demand. For a few of these NCD pastors, the lessons about lifestyle were learned at a high cost. Only one marriage ended because a spouse attended too fully to the demands of the ministry; but several pastors described seasons of marriage that were rough. Marriages and families can break under the strain of NCD work, as one can see from the following testimonies.

> I said that I was having an affair for ten years with the church. And I've since learned and grown from that, but it was really hard. It was difficult. I didn't really realize. I didn't take the time to realize. It's not that I didn't care for [my wife] deeply or our kids, who were really young at the time. It's just that quite often I would spend the best part of [myself] at the church and they got whatever was left, [which was] sometimes just a carcass. (FG 87-89)

> The truth is that the first year in [my NCD] — my marriage almost didn't survive that year. It was one of the most difficult experiences of my life because I felt so called to that place. [I believed] that God really wanted me to be there and be doing what I was doing, and at the same time I was watching my marriage fall apart. [I kept asking,] "How can this be happening?" You know? "How can God al-

low this to take place?" [I was] just struggling with [that] contradictory kind of experience. I think that surviving that [time] was probably the most important thing that ever happened for us and maybe even for the church in terms of identity. (FG 87-89)

I would certainly say that for any pastor there's [always] more work than can be done. And so you pair that with the unknowns of starting a new church. And I think, you know, Type A, whatever you call it, workaholism is a real disease among new church pastors. And our marriage suffered dramatically. (FG 90-93)

Essentially, this profile point is about finding personal and professional balance — and knowing where to set the boundaries for each. Maintaining genuine emotional contact with loved ones and attending to relational depth and growth are challenging enough for any adult. However, for top NCD pastors these demands, coupled with the responsibility to model the Christian life at its best before a watching world of new believers, create very real tensions.

In new-church development you do have some freedom. You begin to shape how that congregation is going to respond to you both as pastor and as married person — or [whatever] the different roles are going to be. In our situation that's been pretty free. I think we have to have a work ethic that respects what Christ has called us to do. But how we are to be in relationship with our spouse and with our children — that can be an example. [We] can show how those relationships can exist in other people's lives as well. We obviously know we cannot work as many hours as we want to every day, every week, and we wouldn't have much to show for it. Probably we wouldn't have [our] personal relationship to show for it. Plus, we're not modeling what God wants for a new relationship — that balance, that perspective. (FG 87-89)

It's kind of a double whammy, in the sense that not only was I spending my best hours in church, but I would come home and there were times where she would have to put me back together because of disappointments, problems, people you just want to shake up, and it's quite a gift that she gave, that I think our [spouses] give. It's quite a gift. (FG 87-89)

Relational health did not stand alone as a general goal. Instead, it was coupled with specific behaviors, such as small-group support and the experience of "iron sharpens iron," that is, one believer calling another to faithfulness and wholeness (Prov. 27:17). These behaviors are more specifically described below:

> I would say the same thing, too. Cutting-edge colleagues — [they are the] number-one resource for me. I would say, in fourteen years that has not changed. (FG 94-96)

> Also, I think that the spiritual and personal life of the missionary pastor must be very, very solid, steadfast, and robust. There are going to be so many challenges that will tempt him [or her] to tear his [or her] marriage apart, his [or her] family, even his [or her] home, [just to follow the NCD call] to walk with the Lord. I think that's real important. (FG 94-96)

> And I think what Jesus was saying is, "I can't give any more until I get fed." Caring for people just saps you. It drains you. (FG 01-02)

> We have a group of us that meet every Monday morning at 7:00, and they're not hesitant to say, "[Pastor], you're full of yourself," or full of something else. And they ask me how my prayer life and how my family life are going. Am I taking time out? Am I studying like I should? It's important for me to have that group. (FG 01-02)

> I had a number of people take me under their wing (Prov. 27:17). (FG 97-00)

These top developers realized that they could not do ministry on their own. Driven by the demands of ministry as much as by their high-energy personalities, they perform a juggling act. They lead full lives in competing worlds — albeit safely, for the most part. Unlike so many leaders who move up the rungs of the career ladder in the helping professions, these leaders do not fly solo. Rather, they resist becoming lone rangers who try to do it all alone: they find supporting spouses, and they find spouse support groups and professional support groups. They nurture the resilience to keep their demanding lives in balance. They set priorities for personal and relational health.

It is particularly noteworthy that the top developers who are women express more concern about the effects of NCD ministry on their children than do their male counterparts, regardless of marital status. Furthermore, women clergy tend to relate more stories of childcare occurring simultaneously with pastoral duties than their male counterparts do. This may indicate that women, even when they are NCD pastors, continue to maintain primary child-rearing responsibilities, despite their spouses' careers. Or perhaps women are more aware of or willing to express their sensitivity to the effects of this particular kind of ministry on the lives of their children.

Passion for Faith-Sharing

Here are the top developers' responses gathered into the fourth category of Tier Two, a "passion for faith-sharing."[17]

- Passion for evangelism and discipleship (2001-2002)
- Networking: willing and desirous to be around unchurched people and contexts; a heart for evangelism, to see people as God sees them (2001-2002)
- Have led someone to Christ; know how to walk with unchurched (2001-2002)
- A passion (or compassion) for people not connected to God (2001-2002)
- Ability to lead others in a study of God's word in a way that moves people forward in their relationship with God (1997-2000)
- Clear vision of who the target group is and how to reach them (1997-2000)
- Believing that Jesus is the only way to life (1987-1989)
- Passion for the lost (1990-1993)
- Commitment to task of reaching out and bringing people into a living relationship with Jesus Christ and his church (1990-1993)

---

17. Responses from post-focus-group questionnaires of top developers: 17 responses, equaling 7 percent of the total citations (same percent as Tier Two profile points of "passion for people," "personal and relational health," and "inspiring preaching and worship").

- Able to be with strangers and make friends on behalf of the gospel (1994-1996)
- Engaging with lost people (1994-1996)
- Boldness in communicating the gospel (1990-1993)
- Teach the people to be there for the lost, not just for themselves (1987-1989)
- Passion for reaching unchurched with the gospel; able to articulate a vision (1994-1996)
- Strong commitment to evangelism: reaching out, seeking out, sharing with non-churched, disaffected, those who have not had experience of God's saving grace (1994-1996)
- Tenacious commitment to share God's word (1987-2002)
- Lively engaging faith — and burning desire to share it (1987-2002)

The survey data provide an illuminating glimpse into the value of spiritual formation for these NCD pastors. Many came from congregations and backgrounds that emphasized evangelism, both in their childhood families and in their home congregations, which — together — served to nurture and shape their initial faith journey. Those whose families and childhood religious experience (within church or parachurch organizations) emphasized evangelism "a great deal" tended to become pastors of the most effective new churches. They are persons who seem most at ease reaching out to unchurched people and sharing the gospel.[18] Surprisingly, these top developers were least likely to say evangelism was emphasized during their seminary years by their seminary, by fellow seminary students, or by the pastors and spiritual mentors available to them during seminary.[19]

18. Survey question Q-24a revealed that pastors of the largest-membership NCDs were 11 percent to 14 percent more likely to come from churches that emphasized evangelism than pastors of lesser membership size. Additionally, according to Q-24b, top developers of the largest-membership churches were 9 percent to 15 percent more likely to come from childhood families that emphasized evangelism "a great deal"; if combined with the qualification "some," they were 14 percent to 24 percent more likely to have had family emphasis on evangelism than did pastors from the smaller-membership churches.

19. Answers from Survey Q-24c, Q-24e, and Q-24f revealed that the top developers registered a lower percentage of evangelism emphasis during seminary years, by the seminaries themselves, by other students, or by pastor/mentors, than did pastors of smaller-membership NCDs. This does not mean that evangelism was not emphasized at all during seminary years, since their answers that combine responses of "a great deal" and "some"

Whether the lack of emphasis on evangelism during seminary serves as an obstacle, which in turn fuels their motivation to succeed, or whether they learn their skills as a "cottage industry" during their formative years without benefit of formal (and more extensive) training, is unknown. What is clear is that these NCD pastors do persist in sharing the gospel. It appears that the childhood home and church home are formative in an effective NCD pastor's understanding of and call to evangelism. It is a call that runs deep, and they do not flag in their zeal to practice evangelism once they are in their NCD pastorate. In fact, they are more likely than smaller-membership pastors to practice evangelism as a continual lifestyle. The most effective NCD pastors are likely, within any ninety-day period, to have assisted a person making a first-time affirmation of faith. Perhaps most surprising, during the period in which data were collected for this study, the top developers reported assisting more persons making a first-time affirmation of faith than the combined total reported by all other pastors of smaller-membership NCDs.[20]

Top developers were least likely to use any denominational evangelism resources to assist people who were making a decision to become a disciple of Christ, though this does not indicate a distaste for institutions and structure. For example, the most effective NCD pastors are more likely to offer a new-member class that shares the vision and direction of the new church than are their less effective counterparts. They also encourage new members to live out a commitment to the institution. They focus on securing sponsors for new members, matching them with mature Christian mentors. They encourage the new disciple to join a small group within the church. These pastors are less likely to emphasize denominational background and traditions to new members. Rather, first and foremost, they emphasize becoming a faithful disciple of Christ in their community of faith.[21]

---

evangelism emphasis for Q-24c, e, f are respectively 43 percent, 33 percent, and 46 percent, with smaller-membership NCD pastors mostly scoring in the 50s and low 60s percentiles.

20. Survey Q-25: the top developers had the highest percentage of evangelism assists at 58 percent; and from Q-26, relating to the same assists question during the last six months, they report the highest number (twenty or more), scoring 12 percent to 22 percent more likely than smaller-membership pastors in assisting with first-time affirmations of faith.

21. Survey Q-27 indicated that the top developers were 50 percent less likely than the smaller-membership NCD pastors to use denominationally generated evangelism

The following statement from a top developer captures this emphasis on evangelism and a vision for the unchurched:

> You have to have a passion for evangelism. It's not enough for me just to [say], "I want to do it for the church, or for myself, or even for the person I'm trying to bring into church." It's got to be, at some point — it's going to be — a passion to bring those people into an eternal relationship with Christ, which is going to completely rock their world and change their eternity and, you know, that's the thing that gets me up when I don't want to go, and that's the thing that gets me moving when I don't want to do it anymore. If that wasn't in there, I would have quit a long time ago. (FG 01-02)

Being passionate about sharing their faith was a common and cultivated skill for the top developers. Like the first followers of Christ after Pentecost, these modern-day apostles teach and witness to Christ's life, death, and resurrection power. The power of the Spirit sent the first disciples out and continues to do so today. Top developers put it this way:

> We set a tone and climate that says, "You are the evangelist in this church; you are called to go out and make very simple, come-and-see invitations, the same way Jesus started the whole thing." Just invite them to come and see. Then we have to trust the Holy Spirit to move when they get here. We can't just be passive about that and say, "Well, you know, hopefully you'll like it." We focused a lot on what people were experiencing in their own lives and still do when they show up the first time. (FG 01-02)

> We were going to reach unchurched people. And do everything in a way that would enable someone who is a Christian to be able to go to someone and invite someone and do it with confidence that if they brought an unchurched person along, that person would

---

materials. In Q-27a, the top developers were head and shoulders above all other NCD pastors (100 percent of the time) in their new-member classes, emphasizing their NCD's vision and direction; twice as likely as smaller-membership NCD pastors to "assign a sponsor to the new members"; and a third more likely than smaller-membership NCD pastors to urge new members to "join a small group." However, the top developers were 10 percent less likely to emphasize "denominational background and traditions" than were smaller-membership NCD pastors.

have a good experience. That was our vision then and it is today. (FG 01-02)

This is the process of church growth — from the ground floor up. The laypeople of these churches, now commissioned to share the good news, catch the passion for faith-sharing and evangelism. Keeping a church out of the maintenance mode (merely running the liturgical and program machinery) means that the faith continues to be passed on from one person to another. Rick Warren describes this evangelical focus in this way:

> I believe you measure the health or strength of a church by its sending capacity rather than its seating capacity. Churches are in the sending business. One of the questions we must ask in evaluating a church's health is, How many people are being mobilized for the Great Commission?[22]

This faith-sharing profile trait is not only invested in top developers' identity but in influence to the congregations they lead. Warren's notion of the "sending capacity" of the NCD is applied from the beginning: new leaders lead toward a mission focus and identity. The effective NCD — and the pastor who leads it — does not reduce the gospel to a sole focus on social justice or community ministries. These churches do more than talk; they are actively engaged in the justice and compassion issues of the secular community. Finally, this "sending" identity was not denominationally driven; rather, it is described by one top developer as "trying to build rapport" with the unchurched:

> Our identity was not who we were as a church denominationally; our identity was trying to build a rapport with two-thirds of the [geographic] area [around us] that didn't go to church anywhere. Even though this area has 160,000 people, they had 250 churches with two-thirds of the population not going. So we built our identity, spent time just getting to know our unchurched friends in the area, building our identity with them. We became an alternative to a lot of other churches; we built a strong rapport with unchurched

22. Rick Warren, *The Purpose-Driven Church* (Grand Rapids: Zondervan, 1995), p. 33.

people, joining other [non-church] organizations and getting known. (FG 87-89)

The ability to develop credibility and connection with the unchurched serves as a key focus in these NCDs. This focus is expressed in three ongoing behaviors: first, it is modeled in a lifestyle composed of faith-sharing by the NCD pastor; second, it is a concept that is woven into the leadership training of laity for evangelism; third, it is emphasized repeatedly in a preaching style that centers on the "basics of the faith" (FG 94-96). An NCD church is one in which members develop Christian maturity by learning to share their journey of faith with the unchurched. Members are encouraged to give the faith away in word and deed to neighbors and church visitors. Hearing the stories of people coming to faith is often part of worship, and it is normative in new-member classes (FG 94-96; FG 97-00).

Again, the vision for faith-sharing seems integrated into the leadership DNA of these effective developers. They teach faith-sharing to their members, and they carefully monitor the "quality control" of the message. Their main intention is for church members to bring unchurched friends confidently to worship or church functions with the assurance that strangers to the church will have a "good experience" (FG 01-02). In short, new churches are a breeding ground for fulfilling the Great Commission. Top developers repeatedly teach their members that they are not "end users of God's grace" or a community of Christ followers that is a closed cul-de-sac (FG 90-93).

In conclusion, the profile trait "passion for faith-sharing" may not stand at the head of the list of NCD leader traits, but it is central to the core paradigm from which these top developers operate. The Holy Spirit uses their passion to bring forth a congregational ethos that reaches the unchurched. This passion for faith-sharing is initiated by a pastor and continued by lay leaders, and it expresses what Jesus taught the first apostles in the Gospel of John, where he clearly defines the steps: "As you [God] have sent me into the world, so I send them into the world," so that the "world may know that you [God] have sent me and have loved them even as you have loved me" (John 17:18, 23).

Inspiring Preaching and Worship

In this last trait of the second-tier grouping, it is important to keep in mind, as with the other second-tier traits mentioned above, that these are coequally weighted profile traits. Here are the responses that created this category:[23]

- Preaching Christ crucified to bring people back into relationship with their Savior (2001-2002)
- Preaching with passion, authenticity, boldness (2001-2002)
- Worship that touches people with the love of God and encourages them on their pilgrim journey (1997-2000)
- Communicating/preaching ability (1997-2000)
- Competence in preaching, leading, caring, and casting vision (1997-2000)
- Preaching skills (1997-2000)
- Always teach and preach the Word; have prayer songs, prayer chains, prayer and praise (Acts 6) (1997-2000)
- Let your sermons and teaching grow out of your own life experiences; find out what God is doing and get in the middle of it (1997-2000)
- A good preacher/communicator/writer (1987-1989)
- Dynamic communicator (1987-1989)
- Passion about Christ; call preaching (1987-1989)
- Effective communicator of God's truths to common, ordinary people, with authenticity, conviction, clarity, both in mass meetings and one-on-one (1994-1996)
- Strong preaching skills (1990-1993)
- Great preaching (1994-1996)
- Able to lead; able to form different worship styles (1987-2002)
- Relevant preaching (1987-2002)
- Strong, broad-based creative worship leadership (1987-2002)

23. Responses from post-focus-group questionnaires of top developers: 17 responses, equaling 7% of the total citations (same percent as Tier Two profile points of "passion for people," "personal and relational health," and "passion for faith-sharing").

Although these two traits — inspiring preaching and worship and a passion for faith-sharing — are discussed as separate skills of these NCD pastors, the separation is false. A more accurate description is that these are intricately woven together; they are the warp and woof of the fabric — indivisible, joined. The traits are equal and coexist in a harmony of traits that are applied at appropriate and different times, depending on the rhythm and flow of the emerging community of faith. As for the importance of inspiring preaching, Galloway captures this idea when he says that "people are not going to listen to a preacher no matter how well [he or she] knows the Bible unless [this person is] a skilled and effective communicator. Before people hear, you must first get their attention . . . in order for the Celebration service to attract people."[24] The top new-church developers are highly skilled communicators who preach the gospel in compelling and attractive ways each Sunday to congregations numbering from the many hundreds to the thousands.

Inspiring preaching can be defined as a Spirit-given gift of "exhortation" and "prophetic word" for the purpose of equipping the laity "for the work of ministry and for building up the body of Christ" (Rom. 12:8; 1 Cor. 12:10; Eph. 4:12). In top developers' worshiping communities, preaching goes hand in hand with inspiring worship. Inspiring preaching and inspiring worship are not just the result of gifted leadership; they take shape in passion fueled by hard work. Preaching and worship are grounded in relationships with worshipers and rooted in a strong and vibrant relationship with God. According to one top developer, the preaching and passion are linked: "Be passionate about your call, about Christ in preaching. . . . You have to preach with a passion . . . taking the truths of God's word that [are] the same yesterday, today, and forever [and] engage [them] in the culture you live in" (FG 87-89). The focus on inspiring preaching and worship forms a "core value" of operational leadership. One may be gifted in preaching, just as athletes are gifted in particular sports; but what separates winners and losers among all gifted athletes is focused energy and hard work. One top developer, commenting on preaching and worship, puts the relationship this way:

24. Galloway, p. 15.

[There is] one belief, one core value that I live by: I'll sit some-times . . . on Sunday morning [and] just watch hundreds of people coming and going and say, "Why did all these people drag them-selves out of bed this morning when they could [have] stayed in bed and watched Schuller? And I really think that — particularly in sub-urbia — people in our congregation, by the time they're thirty or forty years of age, they have tasted what I call all the beverages of life. They've got it all. They've got the houses, the cars, the cabins, the boats. They've been all around the world. They've got every-thing, and yet they know something is missing. I think they come for fellowship, they come for all the programming that we offer for the kids and everything else, but I think, over and above all of that, they come because [outside the church] they have been fed intellec-tually and mentally and physically but not spiritually.

They know there's something missing. And I think as long as we're faithful to that [inspiring preaching and worship] calling, to use the biblical analogy, feed them the Bread of Life, they do come back. They deeply appreciate that and they will come back. We make that [the] focus of the [worship] ministry that we do. (FG 87-89)

These founding pastors shared an equipping vision rooted in a common love for "worship . . . for [leading and] participating in it. It's like 'The Far Side' goes to church, and you are trying to be the body of Christ every single Sunday morning. You have got to love that and what a crazy endeavor it is" (FG 87-02). The energy of an attractive and inviting worship is not just hard work for the preacher; it is centered in what some leaders in the church have abandoned or neglected. Top de-velopers reflect on this:

As the years passed, and as our people matured, we began to see that what people really wanted was a real experience of God. They really wanted to meet God. And you know, the sermons about mar-riage and finances . . . the quality of professional music, they'll go a part of the way, but they have their limits. What people ultimately want is to meet God. (FG 94-96)

What surprised me about people who are de-churched [those who have grown up in the church but are no longer active] is that they expect you to preach on the Bible, and they expect you to use God's name, and they expect you to do a lot of the things that people have completely abandoned. . . . People are hungry for God. I think we have to make God real. We have to let God be what God is for them already. You just unveil this relationship that they long to have and get rid of the boundaries. And we can't do that apart from Scripture. (FG 01-02)

Effective church development in general — and NCD in particular — involves inspiring preaching and worship. It takes practice, hard work, innate giftedness, and — for all preachers — the experience of the Holy. The goal of inspiring worship is an encounter that can be described as a celebration in which both the seeker and mature disciple "meet God" and understand Scripture. The worshipers in these top NCD churches experience preaching that is awash with the Spirit's energy.

Conclusion

Tier-two traits comprise the gifts and skills of preaching, empowering leadership, and the disciplines of relational health. These traits — balance, shared perspectives on mission, passionate focus on the outsider, and the staying power of relational health — fuel the steady movement forward in new communities of faith. Mission communities and evangelism communities do not happen without careful planning and the deployment of skills at appropriate times. It is a process that is supercharged by extraordinary NCD pastors who are aware of the Spirit's empowerment and attentive to the delicate balance of organizational health in the developing community of faith.

Second, this tier addresses a body of learning that is, with one important exception, rarely taught in seminaries or cultivated in traditional parish ministries. That exception is the teaching of preaching and leading in worship, which constitute a traditional part of mainline seminary academics.[25] The remaining skills, however, are virtually ignored in formal training for clergy. Seminary education places little emphasis on how to empower leadership, how to develop a passion for

25. Even in the area of preaching and worship leadership, the art of ministering to the unchurched through worship is often not covered in traditional seminary curricula.

people beyond traditional pastoral care learning, how to nurture a passion for faith-sharing (which few seminaries require in formal training), and how to guard personal and relational health. This study suggests the need for a restructuring or augmenting of some aspects of seminary education. It suggests that cultivating effective clergy who will dedicate themselves to growing the church may require blending theology with training in this unique set of skills.

Third, being able to be the pastor of a church with a large membership does not mean one can automatically become an effective NCD pastor or grow a larger-membership NCD. Starting a church, which grows by reaching formerly unchurched people, is not easy. It requires several simultaneous actions of the NCD pastor: he or she must 1) make quick and effective transitions in leadership style; 2) maintain staying power with a vision of what God's purpose is for the new church; 3) nurture emerging leadership in the congregation; 4) find ways for maturing Christians to feel included; 5) maintain credibility with new believers; and 6) continue to monitor personal and relational health.

Staying on as the pastor of an NCD after developing a formal organization is common practice among effective NCD pastors. To return to the automotive metaphor, if the top-tier traits are the spark plug, and the second-tier traits are the fuel that makes the car run, then the remaining core trait might be called the racing tire: it is the trait that makes for longevity, for effective running power. What leadership abilities are critical for maximum mileage in NCDs? What does a profile of those leaders who "go the distance" and remain effective in missional outreach in the later stages of NCD look like?

The Later Stages of NCD: Beyond Year Seven

The post-focus-group questionnaire asked, "Does the leadership needed in later stages of a church's development differ from the earlier stages? If it does differ, how is that difference displayed?" As noted in Chapter Two, the answer church developers gave to this question is reported as follows:

**Later Stages of New Church Development
(Years 8 through 20)**

Tier 1	Ability to change leadership styles	35%
	Empowering leadership	24%
	Understanding change dynamics	13%
	Vision-casting	8%
		80%
Tier 2	No change	7%
	Other categories (5)[26]	13%
		20%

It is important to note that over one-third of the top NCD founding pastors agreed on the profile point labeled "ability to change leadership styles." Here are the citations that created this final profile point.

Ability to Change Leadership Styles[27]

- It changes to leadership/organization skills from pastoral skills. (1994-1996)
- Sometimes the creative person becomes bored with the administrative choices or the "settled" environment of an established church. (1994-1996)

26. The "other categories" includes five single-digit percentage categories, namely, "ties to a learning community," 4 percent (see page 34 note 5 for definition); "administrative skills," 4 percent; "personal care," 2 percent; "discipleship training," 2 percent; and "humility," 1 percent.

27. Responses from post-focus-group questionnaires of top developers: 29 responses (equaling 35 percent of the total citations) given to the question "Does the leadership needed in later stages of a church's development differ from the early stages? If so, how?" The survey developed only one profile point from this section of questionnaire responses because the next-highest-level response was a continuation of leadership style noted earlier in the profile, namely, "empowering leadership," with twenty responses and accounting for 23 percent of the answers; then "understanding change dynamics," with eleven responses and equaling 13 percent of the answers; and "vision casting," with seven responses and equaling 8 percent of the answers. After these responses, the final answers do not constitute a statistically important category or variable.

- Ability to recognize the need to think more administratively, to add and use gifts of other staff (1994-1996)
- Cannot be one-on-one with everyone as before (1994-1996)
- It is critical to develop and train a large number of lay leaders and to adapt leadership style to fit a significantly more complex organization with an increasing number of members. (1994-1996)
- "Hands on" to "hands off" (1990-1993)
- Inspirational to apostolic (1990-1993)
- It is exactly the same as the early stages; what will change is the role of the leader in the life of the congregation. (1987-1989)
- The challenge of leading a more complex organization is that it requires a more consultative and less directive approach. (1997-2000)
- Other later competencies: organizational skills and staff leadership (1997-2000)
- Staff leadership (1997-2000)
- We need increasingly to be leaders and not doers of ministry. (1997-2000)
- Learning how to lead and manage stuff becomes very important. (1987-1989)
- Catalytic to organizational (1990-1993)
- Many components are the same, but the issue is: will the mission developer maintain the passion for seeing the growing church as a vital work as he originally did, even though a lot more of it is visible? (1994-1996)
- Must be able to transition from "solo" pastor to working with a multiperson staff (1987-1989)
- Must develop administrative skills (1987-1989)
- Must understand how to change with different organizational sizes (1997-2000)
- Become more crucial/intensive (2001-2002)
- Change is easier in the early stages; leader must work through more channels and in different ways as the church grows. (1997-2000)
- Need to focus specifically on developing leadership skills in specific areas: staff development, organizational communications, and promoting unity in the midst of rapid growth (2001-2002)
- More from leading volunteers to leading staff (2001-2002)

- As the congregation grows and the dynamics change, it is important to recognize how the pastor's role is changing with it. The pastor must be able to see the transitions that the congregation needs to make in order to continue to grow, and must support those changes. (2001-2002)
- You still need boundaries, maybe even more so, because you're redefining your role and you need to stay within the new role. (1987-2002)
- Move from developer to transformer (1987-2002)
- Go from the person who does everything to a training and delegating model (1987-2002)
- Alban's understanding of the change from pastoral and programmatic leadership style (1987-2002)
- After a core group is formed, the congregation is organized [over 100 in worship]; the pastor needs to adapt from high developer skills to pastoral skills as needed. (1987-2002)
- Pastor needs to use different management styles at various stages of the congregation's life/growth if he or she remains in the call. That's why some pastors are great starters and may or may not be able to adapt for the needs of next stages. (1987-2002)

It is clear that, as church membership grows and stabilizes, these pastors begin to modify their leadership styles. Their work and management styles change as they redefine congregant administration needs. In short, what separates these top developers from those who are otherwise effective but who leave after the seventh year (or those who pastor smaller-membership NCDs) is that top developers recognize the transitions taking place in the life of a congregation. These top NCD developers learn to adapt and facilitate growth in membership transitions; it means that they learn to refine — even redefine — their roles. They frequently are involved in engaging a new staff. There are new teams of people moving through growth barriers, and the barriers come with ever-increasing numbers of worshipers and new members. Learning to adapt to emerging and complex organizational structures, deploying members on the basis of spiritual giftedness while infusing them with expertise and enthusiasm, and knowing when to delegate specific tasks of ministry are the hallmarks of change in their leadership style. Not a single NCD pastor mentioned taking a seminary course in how to make these changes in a growing congregation. Instead, they run on intuition. They make changes in leadership styles boldly when they sense that the time is right. The following are samples of what they said in the focus groups:

> The freedom to dream, staying close to that dream with God — and one beauty that I love about mission development — is how it doesn't have a total structure and power system set to it. It is so open and so free, and one of the advantages is that you can change gears. (FG 87-02)

> The key to longevity in ministry and the key to going through this process is the ability to change your ministry style as the size of the congregation grows. If you can't do that, the church either will stop growing or you'll be gone. The flexibility of leadership — I think it's critical. (FG 87-89)

> I think the biggest barrier to church growth is the pastor who can't [adapt]. For me, the issue is control. I see so many guys who just can't get out of the way. They can't give the ministry away, and that's when the church shuts down. The church will grow to the size where they . . . can't manage it and be in control. And that's it. I'm quite confident around here that every one of us has given ministry away. The business of my ministry I have changed. I have a certain number of gifts, and I continue to redefine myself so I'm staying in my gift area and looking for staff people to complement that and grow the church in that way. (FG 87-89)

> Even if you stay in a place, you have to reinvent yourself every five to seven years. You have to be thinking — who am I as a leader? What is this pastime? What has this past project done to me and my family? (FG 97-00)

Embracing change has its own set of devils. Change requires humility when success comes, when worship attendance and membership size are significantly larger than established congregations within the same denomination and locality. The church is not the only place that is resistant to change. What separated top founding pastors from other NCD pastors is true for executives in complex and growing organizations. According to Peter Drucker, "The most common executive failure is inability or unwillingness to change with the demands of a new position."[28] The evidence of this study of top developers is that leadership style changed and so did the organization of the church. Being able to change — that is, to reinvent oneself at the critical places of membership growth — is difficult, but these leaders did change — and their change was not capricious or rapid.

Change is particularly hard if the change hits one at the core. Yet substantive change in old (and cherished) patterns was just what these top developers did as the Spirit was adding "day by day to the number of those being saved" (Acts 2:47). Coupled with the first- and second-tier traits, this ability to change leadership styles adds a distinctive profile point.

*   *   *

We turn now to a concluding postscript, which juxtaposes the profile points from Chapters Two and Three with the "gifts of leadership in ministry" that Robert Hoyt identifies in Appendix A.

Profile Traits and Gifts of Leadership

Wood's Leadership Profile	*Hoyt's "Gifts of Leadership"*
Catalytic innovator	
Charismatic leader	Passion for this work
Tenacious perseverer	High expectations
Risk-taker	Willingness to risk
Flexible adapter	Willingness to let people go
Self-starter	Flexibility, adaptability, and change as the congregation grows
Abiding faith in God	Focus on Jesus
	Mission is at the center of life
	Prayer is at the center of life
Visionary/vision-caster	Vision- and mission-driven
	Developing and respecting core values
	Developing identity

28. Peter Drucker, *The Effective Executive* (New York: Harper Collins, 1966), p. 58.

Empowering leadership   Building and experiencing
                                  Christian community
                               Staffing as team building
                               Building lay ministry
                               Equipping people for ministry
                               Respecting diversity
Passion for people   Respecting people
                               Knowing your community
                               Developing local ownership
Personal and relational health Building personal relationships
                               Going beyond a personal rela-
                                  tionship with the pastor
Passion for faith-sharing   This ministry is a "God thing"
                               A spiritual relationship with
                                  God
Inspiring preaching and worship

Profile of Pastoral Leadership Changes over Time

Ability to change leadership   Humility and a willingness to
   styles   learn from others
                               Leaders multiply ministry by
                                  giving it away
                               Shared authority

There is considerable — though not complete — correlation between the "profile traits" and the "gifts of leadership in ministry." The
gifts of the NCD pastors add clarity and first-hand testimony, which
can be used in coaching seminary students and emerging new-church
pastors. Initially, the NCD developer is a key factor in "birthing" the
emerging congregation, and he or she champions the vision for God's
kingdom in the context of the community. Although no "gift" is assigned for the profile trait of "inspiring preaching and worship leader,"
this may be understood as implicit in effective NCD start-ups and absolutely vital in the later stages of development.

A few conclusions can be drawn from these data. First, many
clergy effectively pastor churches that are well established when they
begin the pastorate. However, NCD denominational executives unani-

mously agree that, in any seminary class, there are only a few pastors who have the particular mix of gifts and skills to start an effective NCD. Not many candidates currently recruited and nurtured by seminary faculty are trained to reach formerly unchurched persons and incorporate them into an ongoing body of believers who visibly demonstrate God's kingdom.

Second, identifying these traits serves as an aid to identifying and calling these pastors. These candidates may find the call to an NCD pastorate to be an ideal one. Third, there is reason to rejoice that so many different denominations have partnered to provide these data. It is doubtless a harbinger of further partnering to provide deeper study of this unique constellation of gifts, skills, and behaviors. If the last few decades are instructive in matters of church growth, this study certainly contributes to a growing body of knowledge suggesting that church leaders in the twenty-first century will be decreasingly defined by denominational identity. As the focus continues to expand in the ways and means of reaching the unchurched with the gospel, the identification and understanding of those who are best equipped to do the work make a significant contribution to our understanding of how the Holy Spirit is at work in our world. These extraordinary pastors truly embody "the precious message" of the gospel in the "unadorned clay pots" of their ordinary lives. It is from their work and skill — yet humble transparency — that the "brightness" of God's power is demonstrated (2 Cor. 4:7 [*The Message* translation]).

Chapter Four

What Makes a Difference in FACT?

CARL S. DUDLEY

Developing new congregations requires leaders with a unique but elusive array of personality traits, professional competencies, and faith commitments. Defining these characteristics was the object of the research in the multi-denominational study entitled "New Church Development for the 21st Century" (NCD), the results of which Stan Wood has discussed in the previous two chapters. In this chapter I will compare the results of this NCD study with responses from a larger set of data developed at about the same time from a study entitled "Faith Communities Today" (FACT).

NCD provides survey data from 704 new-church-development pastors, plus qualitative data from six focus groups of extraordinary NCD pastors from seven Protestant denominations. The ambitious goal of this research is to identify characteristics that could be used to select and train successful NCD pastors. In contrast, FACT gathered information from 14,301 congregations in forty-one faith communities (more than 90 percent of the regular worship attendance in the United States), but with a more global focus on congregational life — from buildings and parking lots to spiritual growth and social outreach. In survey data, both studies depend on information from key informants, and both are made possible by funding from the Lilly Endowment and the participating faith groups.

As an interfaith study, FACT presents information from a wide spectrum of faith communities, from Methodists and Mennonites to Mormons and Muslims; it includes Jews, Roman Catholics, and Orthodox Christians, as well as evangelical, mainline, and historically black Protestant churches. These congregations were drawn from the landscape of American religious groups, large and small, rural and metropolitan, old and recently organized. (The results of the full study can be accessed through the FACT website at www.fact.hartsem.edu, which includes links to a wide variety of published reports primarily written by participating faith communities.)

The fundamental difference between the NCD study and the FACT study is as follows: the NCD study focuses on leadership characteristics, while this chapter's FACT survey focuses on information about congregations as a whole. In a sense, NCD looks "down from the top," beginning with the leaders who shape the church, while FACT looks "up from the bottom," beginning with the congregation and then asking what kind of leader would produce this result. Since the focus of the two studies was singularly different, the similarities we have discovered seem even more significant.

The organization of this chapter is based on NCD hypotheses, but the emphases have been restated and rearranged to reflect seven parallel findings in FACT. At some points the data affirm and expand the findings of Hoyt and Wood, but sometimes there are alternative and even challenging readings to the NCD results. In this limited space the data will speak to the issues raised in the NCD-FACT comparisons through a combination of cross-tabulations in figures and brief commentary, along with quotes from the NCD survey and the focus-group responses. For example, when we compare the FACT findings with the chapters by Wood, the importance of a shared "vision" dominates the data from all studies. Also, a "passion for people" is an irrepressible element of successful leaders, and "empowering leadership" is central to successful leadership throughout. The importance of "worship" is pivotal; but note that worship is treated differently in the two surveys: NCD emphasizes dimensions of personal faith, while FACT examines the cultural and generational differences that shape worship experiences. Clearly, the chemistry of charisma is significant, but that is also interpreted differently in the two studies: FACT examines several dimensions of "flexibility," "conflict," and "change," while Hoyt and Wood choose a variety of other lenses — such as "professional risk" or "adapting to shared authority."

In the data presentation of this chapter, the avalanche of information from comparing two extensive studies may overwhelm readers and make application to practical issues difficult. For that reason, readers may wish to select areas of particular interest and take time to reflect on the implications of these data. Such implications might be shaped in the following reflective questions: Do these findings agree with my experience? Do they explain problems and issues we have experienced? What differences might these findings make in how we now select, prepare, and support new-church-development pastors?

In summary, these seven findings from FACT are listed as broad themes with numerous possible implications:

I. **Location: Demographics define your opportunity**
   A. Choose your location carefully
   B. Niche: focus on specific people
   C. Niche: focus on families
   D. Niche: ethnic and immigrant congregations
   E. Niche: multicultural outreach

II. **Vision: Sharing purpose makes the difference**
   A. Vision mobilizes energy
   B. Vision increases commitment
   C. Vision struggles with age
   D. Vision must match location

III. **Relationships: Caring for members and neighbors**
   A. Build community among members
   B. Care for your neighbors

IV. **Size matters — but people, not programs, build churches**
   A. Expect more in larger churches
   B. Demand more from larger churches
   C. Use growth energy for more growth

V. **Worship: Inspiring, relevant worship accompanies growth**
   A. Generations reflect real differences
   B. Make innovation relevant

VI. Flexibility: Fixed plans must bend or break
   A. Use generational differences creatively
   B. Older churches must change more
   C. Make conflict work for you

VII. Education fails: Leadership is caught, not taught
   A. We cannot teach charisma
   B. Creative teachers can be nurtured

Introduction

Congregations in the FACT study placed great emphasis on membership growth. Fifty-one percent of the participating congregations reported 5 percent or more membership growth in the past five years, while 31 percent reported membership plateau, and 19% reported declining membership (Fig. 1). Since FACT is a broad interfaith study, the high percentage of churches that claim growth reflected far greater vitality throughout religious institutions than previously anticipated.

This high level of interest in growth offers a parallel to the participants in the NCD study. The 704 congregations were selected because they were new-church starts that were designed for growth, and the participants in the focus groups were chosen because they were particularly effective and articulate in the church-growth process.

A careful review of FACT data suggests a slight "halo effect." Key informants of congregations in some established Protestant denominations reported slightly larger numbers (about 1 percent) than they reported on other data from within their own denominations, such as annual reports. Such a small and documented shift in data suggests the importance of membership growth and a desire to offer the most favorable interpretation of their situation. The same "halo effect" may be true of the NCD data as well. The shift must be acknowledged as we explore the importance and the implications for leadership in church growth. These congregational leaders want to see themselves as growing, and they intend to do what is necessary to help it happen.

Carl S. Dudley

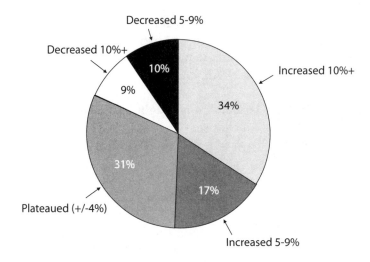

Figure 1. % Congregations Growing/Declining

Location: Demographics Define Your Opportunity

A. *Choose Your Location Carefully*

"Location, location, location" — the top three reasons for successful real estate listings and purchases are apparently applicable to church growth as well. The pivotal importance of demographics in congregational location has been well documented in the NCD study.[1] As the NCD hypothesis predicted, congregational growth is far more likely in new suburban communities. The demographics were also reflected in the focus-group conversations with new-church pastors. For them, community demographics was central. One pastor said, "Build a community where population growth is really dynamic." A second pastor

---

1. Survey Q-56: 50 percent of the largest and fastest-growing churches were in "new suburbs of a large city," three times higher than the second-fastest-growing area (14 percent). Survey Q-57: 90 percent of the largest and fastest-growing churches were in areas of "significant population growth," compared to 56 percent of smaller congregations (under 100 members). [All Q's refer to the New Church Development survey.]

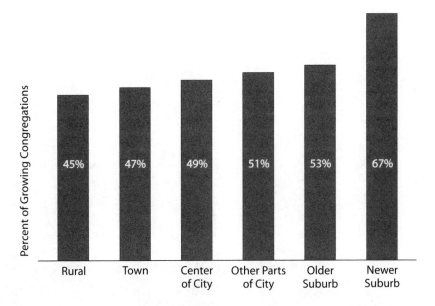

Figure 2. Location and Growth

agreed: "It's good demographics!" A third pastor summed it up with, "Yeah, pick your demographics carefully" (FG 87-89).

But location is a mindset more than a place. As Donald McGavran has noted, restless populations are more responsive to evangelical appeals.[2] Even allowing for extra enthusiasm in numerical reporting, significant growth is occurring among mobile people in every location (Fig. 2). Rural areas, as well as smaller towns where populations are declining, still have room for creative pastors and industrious congregations. With focus, commitment, and the grace of God, church growth can happen anywhere people are restless and willing to make changes. This report suggests various ways that congregations can grow with or without a favorable social context.

2. See Donald McGavran, *Understanding Church Growth* (Grand Rapids: Eerdmans, 1970), pp. 152ff.

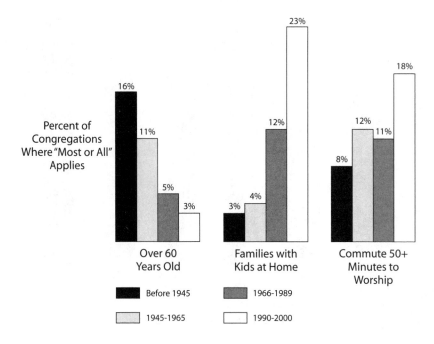

Figure 3. Older and Newer Congregations

B. Niche: Focus on Specific People

When the NCD study is set in a larger framework, we recognize the advantages inherent in new beginnings. New-church starts can choose locations where they have access to younger members, who in turn are more likely to have growing families. Further, as a mark of changing times, members of newly formed churches are as willing to commute to church as they do to their employment; hence these congregations can draw from a larger catch basin.

It is a common new-church planning strategy not to focus on the place or the people in general, but to decide on specific target population(s). New churches that target the entire community are generally not as effective as new churches that choose a carefully selected group of people they feel they will have the capacity to serve. Selecting a particular slice of the population is consistent with Donald McGavran's

controversial "homogeneous unit principle,"[3] which urges development pastors to minimize the social and language barriers that people
have to cross to become Christians and join the church.

This social affinity helps both the group and the pastor appreciate and share their common culture. In this awareness of shared family
values, it is common for a brochure on new-church development to
show a picture of the church planter's whole family, to encourage and
build a common cultural foundation. Pastors interviewed often spoke
of their focus on "the perceived needs of the community, both the spiritual needs of people, you know, their socio-economic level, makeup of
the households, what's going to be your mission in the community"
(FG 90-93).

C. Niche: Focus on Families

Families provide the most common niche population for new congregations. The appeal of the suburban location lies in the many ways
that congregations can serve the needs of growing families. Congregational strategies are often geared to assist families as they first enter new neighborhoods with childcare and educational programs,
with religious instruction, character building, sports and health
events, and a wide variety of cultural expressions. These not only
serve community needs but also allow newcomers to be socialized
into neighborhood networks of essential information, gossip, and
normative expectations. In the accompanying graph (Fig. 4), the
growth of congregations rises in direct proportion to the number of
families in the community, except in areas where families number in
excess of 80 percent. There are few of these areas, and they are unusu-
ally dense — such as massive housing complexes. In general, large
housing complexes with many rental units have a mobile population
that is more difficult to reach than are families in areas where home
ownership is high.

NCD data strongly support the careful selection of communities
with more favorable circumstances for success. Larger and growing
congregations consistently engaged in extensive demographic study,

3. McGavren, *Church Growth*, pp. 190ff.

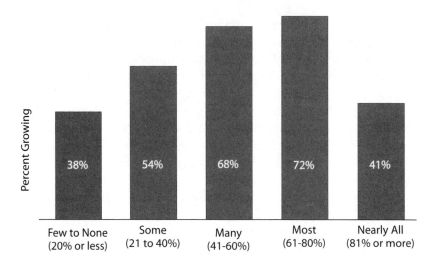

Figure 4. % Households with Children and Growth

compared with smaller churches (56 percent vs. 31 percent).[4] Although the numbers of this report are unusual, the comment below is typical:

> [Town name] . . . growth has been phenomenal. We have about 150 families a month moving into town. That's been going on for about seven years now, and it doesn't seem to show any sign of stopping. . . . We just celebrated our fourth anniversary in September. Our membership is right around 600. (FG 01-02)

D. Niche: Ethnic and Immigrant Congregations

Demographics are as much about people as about place. In an age in which denominational differences have been reportedly declining, FACT data show that two-thirds of participating congregations believe that they are expressing their denominational heritage very well or

4. Survey Q-9: 56 percent of the largest and fastest-growing congregations say church leaders report extensive demographic study, while only 31 percent of the smallest congregations make comparable claims.

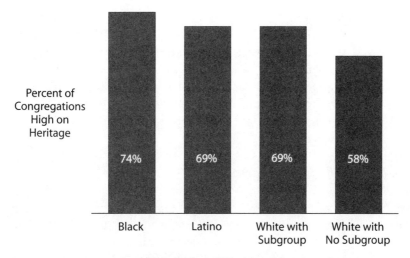

Figure 5. Majority Race / Ethnicity of Congregation

Figure 5. Majority Race / Ethnicity and Denominational Heritage

quite well. Language, ethnicity, race, and culture are intimately inter-woven with denominational heritage as a backbone of identity in many congregations, as suggested in the accompanying graph (Fig. 5).

New-church development and growth in many areas will depend on the leaders' skill in building on denominational heritage as a posi-tive strength without creating exclusive enclaves that deny access to other potential members. Here and throughout this study, NCD survey hypotheses that organizing pastors "should focus on major population groups in their community" have been supported by NCD data show-ing that, in the largest and fastest-growing congregations, the social contacts of existing church members are by far the largest source for prospective new members.[5]

Although established church cultures are often so entrenched that they find it difficult to adapt their patterns and habits to accom-

5. Survey Q-31e: 50 percent of the largest and growing congregations say their members were a major source for unchurched prospects, compared to under half that number in other groups.

modate new groups, some denominational strategies have specifically targeted such groups: "[We have] a commitment to start one new-church development per year, and we have been doing that with an explosion of racial/ethnic startups. [Church name] is about a 550-member congregation. Music has been a strong factor, multiple staff, weekday preschool program, part-time youth, full-time DCE, senior pastor, part-time music staff — a variety of folk" (FG 94-96).

E. Niche: Multicultural Outreach

It helps to consider all new church development as cross-cultural ministry. This can be true even when the target group is similar in demographic characteristics to the denomination reaching out to them, such as a mainline Protestant church effort to reach a suburban, middle-class, largely white population. That is, all new-church development is about doing church for people for whom church is outside the comfortable habits of their lives.

At the same time, some congregations want to do more. On the basis of the belief that the gospel transcends social, racial, and ethnic distinctions (Gal. 3:28), some new churches focus on a particular group of people in order to reach the critical mass necessary to sustain the new congregation. From that base they move to include other, more varied populations. Even burdened with the entrenched cultural foundations associated with denominational heritage, urban diversity redefines some religious traditions to be more inclusive. Congregations in urban areas are far more likely to encourage and pursue racial diversity in their membership than are congregations in more rural and town communities (Fig. 6). Therefore, population availability directly affects how congregations respond to cultural differences.

One urban pastor recalls: "We had never articulated as part of our vision that we would be a multi-ethnic church. But we discovered God was leading us in that direction. To the point where we asked someone who was Anglo, 'Why did you choose [our] church?' and he said, 'Because of the variety here, you know, I wanted to come to a multi-ethnic church'" (FG 94-96).

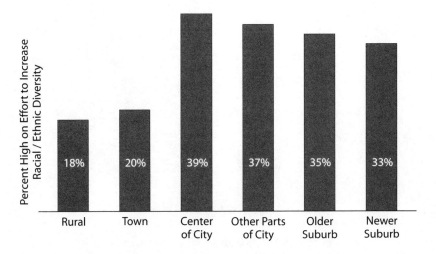

Figure 6. Effort to Increase Diversity and Location

Vision: Sharing Purpose Makes the Difference

F. Vision Mobilizes Energy

"Vision" commonly describes a carefully planned ministry statement that includes a specific mental picture of a preferable future, a purpose statement that explains why the new church exists (sometimes called a mission statement), and a summary of the core ministry values. Out of the vision, purpose, and value statements follow the goals and strategies used to develop the new congregation.

In the FACT study we find strong support for the NCD hypothesis that effective church builders "need to articulate a compelling vision for the ministry." In the FACT data, no correlation with growth is stronger than that. Congregations with clear, positive vision also express strong internal vitality. Conversely, congregational observers who see only an implicit mission or little clarity of vision feel the congregation is low in expressing vitality. Since vision and vitality correlate with other factors differently throughout the FACT study, we are not simply examining the same item from two perspectives. Vitality and vision are mutually dependent (see Fig. 7).

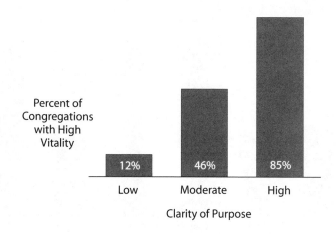

Percent of
Congregations
with High
Vitality

12%   46%   85%

Low   Moderate   High

Clarity of Purpose

Figure 7. Vitality and Clarity of Purpose

Throughout the interviews, NCD leaders report the foundational importance of a shared vision. In the NCD data, the largest and fastest-growing churches were more likely than the smaller congregations (43 percent vs. 14 percent) to report that the congregation shares the vision for the church's future "exactly."[6] Interviews showed the deep feelings beneath these statistics, as one pastor pointed out: "You need to embody the vision. You need to communicate the vision. You need to be passionate about the vision. You need to drive old cars because you care that much about the vision" (FG 90-93).

G. Vision Increases Commitment

In the NCD focus groups, "vision" is the most frequently discussed characteristic of growing churches. Says one pastor, "I need to know that whatever happens fits within the overall purpose of why we exist, and if it doesn't, then we ought to sit down and talk about doing it. In other words, we need to have focus to everything we do" (FG 87-89).

6. Survey Q-31b: 43 percent of the largest and growing congregations say church leaders share "exactly" the same vision for the church's future, while only 14 percent of the smallest congregations make comparable claims.

Shared vision is directly related to the energy of commitment in the congregation. Vision allows leaders to expect more from their members, and in turn the members have the satisfaction of achieving more as a group. In the FACT study, clarity of vision is associated with the strictness of member expectations in the patterns of growing congregations (Fig. 8). A similar finding is reflected in the NCD study, where 100 percent of the new-member classes in the fastest-growing congregations affirmed the vision and direction of the congregation.[7] In these churches, members indicated significantly more involvement in the ministry,[8] and were more likely to act as sponsors for new members.[9] Clearly, shared vision is synonymous with commitment. One pastor observed:

> Vision is a very important thing. . . . We made a decision early on that we were not going to be a membership congregation; we were going to be a discipleship congregation. So I've never focused on membership . . . but we have focused on making disciples and covenanting to be a disciple. . . . Rather than thinking, "Well, I can come in, sign this piece of paper, I'm a member, and now I can sit back and relax." [This church] is not a health club where you pay your dues and come whenever you feel like it. It only happens because of your presence and your commitment to ministry. (FG 01-02)

H. Vision Struggles with Age

Beyond the young congregations in the NCD study, the FACT data provide a unique perspective on what happens to congregational clarity of purpose over the years. Over time, it seems, "vision declines with age," and this happens to congregations as well as individuals. Over the years the sense of purpose seems to become less explicit and more im-

7. Survey Q-35: 100 percent of the largest and growing congregations say their "vision and direction were presented to new members," significantly higher than in all other groups of congregations.

8. Survey Q-31: 61 percent of the largest and growing congregations say that members are "directly involved in ministry activities," significantly higher than all other groups of congregations.

9. Survey Q-33a: 30 percent of the largest and growing congregations say a "sponsor is always assigned to each new member," compared to 10 percent of the smallest churches.

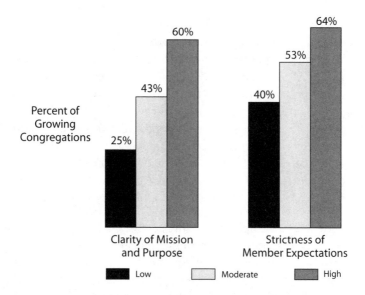

Figure 8. Clarity / Strictness and Growth

plicit, assumed and "commonly understood." Process dynamics suggest that, as organizations age, their primary purpose becomes survival. Further, the layers of several generations may make the simple clarity of vision more difficult. Older congregations have more difficulty in agreeing on clarity of focus in ministry (Fig. 9).

Congregations have a natural aging process. They are born, grow, and mature, and they will decline and die unless values and procedures are put in place to keep renewing the congregational vitality. We can see from the NCD study that the pastors in the largest and fastest-growing congregations are giving a higher priority to "clearly articulating a vision for the congregation" and constantly renewing their goals and objectives, as compared to leaders in smaller churches.[10] Young

10. Survey Q-40d: 71 percent of the pastors in the largest and growing congregations give priority to "clearly articulating a vision for the congregation," compared to 47 percent in smaller churches. Survey Q-40e: 64 percent of the pastors in the largest and growing congregations say they give priority to "developing goals and objectives," compared to 35 percent in smaller churches.

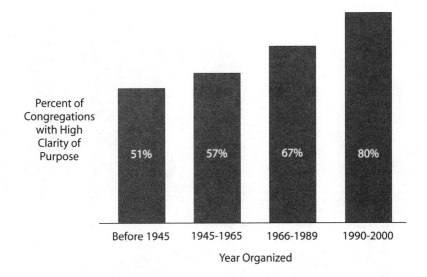

Figure 9. Clarity and Year Organized

congregations should examine the habits of congregational self-evaluation and build in a commitment to critical review and periodic renewal. One participant summarized the feelings of many: "The tenacity of holding on to that vision and holding it before your people, protecting it when you must and protecting it from being hijacked into sort of a maintenance mode, is something I certainly hear in every voice in this room" (FG 97-00).

I. Vision Must Match Location

Location also makes a difference in the clarity of mission. In the short life and relative simplicity of new suburbs, congregational mission can seem more explicit, clear, and focused. However, as communities — like congregations — age, mature, and grow older, the location itself makes it more difficult to achieve a single shared vision of congregational mission (Fig. 10). Both age and location need to be taken into account as pastors seek to achieve a clear sense of mission with congregational leaders.

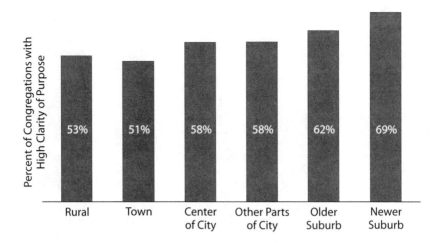

Figure 10. Clarity and Location

Compelling vision is specific and takes into account the particular niche within the community where the church is located. One pastor made these decisions quite specific: "I started the church in 1989, and we're a multi-ethnic group, probably about 50 to 60 percent Anglo, probably about 25 to 30 percent Hispanic, and the rest would be a mixture of African-American and Asian. . . . I was interested in Southern California because I thought that it would be most fertile for a multi-ethnic church" (FG 94-96).

At the same time, it is not unusual for a long-established church to overlook the community changes that have been taking place all around it until the changes begin to show in the aging of the congregation — and they impact attendance and income. Pastors in the largest and fastest-growing congregations made special efforts to keep their members involved and informed.[11] Growing churches are able to discern the needs of neighbors, and they may alter their vision and strategies to match changing populations and community circumstances.

11. Survey Q-39: 29 percent of the pastors in larger congregations place priority on "inspiring and motivating members to be involved in the community," compared to under half that number of pastors in smaller churches.

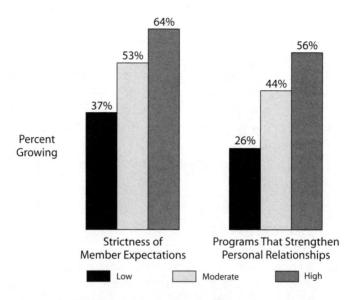

Figure 11. Strictness and Personal Relations = Growth

Relationships: Caring for Members and Neighbors

J. Build Community among Members

The affirmation that relationships are central to church growth weaves together several NCD hypotheses with a slightly different emphasis. In numerous questions, the NCD study explored the important role of clergy to disciple new members to become ministry participants. As noted above, we have seen the positive impact of high membership expectations when the vision is clear and the purpose widely shared. At the same time, we see in the FACT data a parallel emphasis on relationships, on caring among members within the congregation. As seen in FACT (Fig. 11), strictness of membership is sustained and strengthened by personal relationships. Members are more willing to act on high expectations in a context of personal affection and support. High demands without strong social networks are counterproductive and usually produce negative effects.

Because small groups are so much a part of every church, congregations of all sizes report similar levels of commitment, creating personal relationships in small groups and various church activities. The difference appears to be this: growing congregations are more intentional. For example, 82 percent of the largest and fastest-growing congregations report that they have an "intentional, systematic attempt to track visitors, contacts and other prospects," compared to 43 percent of the smaller congregations. Furthermore, growing churches are three times more likely to always assign a sponsor to each new member.[12] Apparently, growing churches invest more in making relationships succeed.

K. Care for Your Neighbors

In addition to caring about members within, relationships with neighbors in the community also provide energy and an avenue for evangelistic outreach. This characteristic of building relationships through community outreach is not evident in the first years of new-church development, as suggested by several neutral and negative correlations in the NCD study.[13] But as congregations mature, even the NCD data suggest a positive correlation between community relationships and congregational size.[14]

FACT responses suggest that growing congregations are more directly and continuously in touch with their communities, based on the number of different social programs sponsored by the church; and, perhaps more controversial, these data show a correlation between membership growth and congregational commitment to work for social jus-

12. Survey Q-31f: 82 percent of the largest and growing congregations report that they have an "intentional, systematic attempt to track visitors, contacts, and other prospects," compared to 43 percent in smaller congregations. Survey Q-33a: 30 percent of the largest and growing congregations say that a "sponsor is always assigned to each new member," compared to 10 percent of the smallest churches.

13. For example, Survey Q-22g, Q-30c, Q-37f, Q-39f all show no difference or a negative correlation with growth by congregations that engage in community ministries in the early years.

14. Survey Q-31d: Over time, however, 75 percent of the largest and growing congregations were described as having "had numerous contacts with the local community," compared to 58 percent of smaller churches.

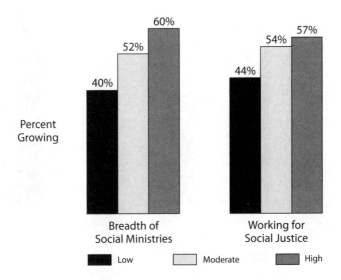

Figure 12. Growth and Breadth of Ministry / Social Justice

tice (Fig. 12). One pastor explained: "There really were two concepts that stayed with me. . . . One is affluence and the other one is alienation. And I saw that everywhere. And that formed the need for the community and the need to serve, to get outside yourself" (FG 90-93).

In combining these pastors' focus groups with the wide range of congregations in FACT, these data suggest that social outreach ministries appear more likely to support growth as churches mature and settle in their communities.

Size Matters — but People, Not Programs, Build Churches

L. Expect More in Larger Churches

The desire to find leaders who can create large churches — even megachurches — is understandable. From every organizational aspect, larger congregations look better. FACT research found that larger congregations had many more programs, while members of smaller con-

Carl S. Dudley

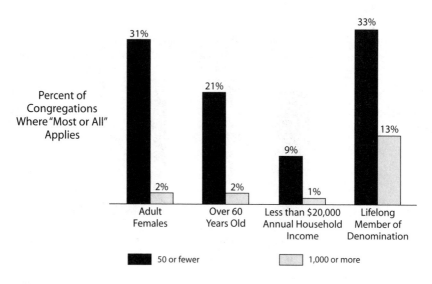

Figure 13. Comparison of Smallest and Largest Congregations

gregations reported more satisfying personal relations (which may explain why some small churches are less interested in growth). But we need to face the differences between small and large more directly. The profile of a typical small church (under 50 members) shows that it has few resources for significant growth. It is often dominated by women who are over sixty years old, have few financial resources, and are likely to be lifelong members of that denomination (Fig. 13). Such a congregation may be healthy and caring, but it is highly unlikely to show rapid, significant membership growth, regardless of programs or leadership skills.

The NCD survey,[15] along with participating denominational information, showed that the size of the first meeting of the congregation set the stage for growth. Consistently, the strongest correlate of new-

15. Survey Q-4: 44 percent of the largest and growing congregations report 125 or more in attendance at their first public worship, compared to only 13 percent of the smaller congregations. Survey Q-5: 76 percent of the largest and growing congregations had 90 or more in attendance in worship after 3 months, compared to 9 percent of the smaller congregations.

118

church success was the number in attendance at the first meeting. Congregations that had 75+ in worship attendance at the outset (by the third month) grew to be the largest and strongest; those that began with fewer than 40 remained small. This "rule of thumb" would seem to be the most consistent measure by which denominational decision-makers could risk additional funding. This also forms the greatest challenge that NCD pastors must confront at the threshold of their ministry.

M. Demand More from Larger Churches

Leadership in a larger church demands a different kind of approach than guiding a smaller congregation. In the larger churches, the lead pastor tends to be a visionary and pacesetter (as discussed above) who gets energized by people and has significantly more energy than pastors of smaller congregations.[16] Further, the FACT study shows that larger churches are more likely to experiment with alternative approaches and are more apt to purchase materials from nondenominational sources (whatever fits the need). Larger congregations have more to work with, and they do more with what they have. As a result, they feel much better about their financial resources, and they feel far less strain in finding enough volunteers to get the job done (Fig. 14). FACT research (not shown) indicates that larger churches have more diversity of programs: it is an effort to provide something for every segment of the church. Thus, larger churches have greater "economies of scale," which provide greater selectivity to those searching for faith, belonging, and growth. Nevertheless, greater size can be a detriment to those wishing to experience loving relationships in the community of faith — even in the presence of a system of strong relational groups.

16. Survey Q-36h: 63 percent say they get "energized by being with people," compared to 45 percent in other groups. Survey Q-36f: 67 percent of pastors in the largest and growing congregations report that they have "energy to take on additional tasks," almost twice the level of response from other congregational groups.

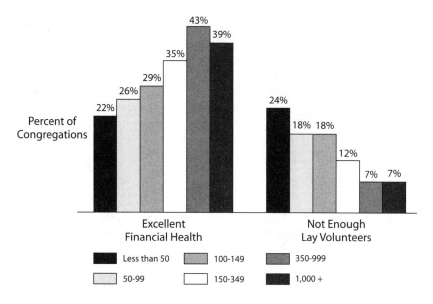

Figure 14. Finance / Volunteers and Size

N. Use Growth Energy for More Growth

The NCD research has appropriately emphasized the critical mass, that larger congregations can allocate more resources and creativity to evangelistic tasks. Bigger can be better; but there is no compelling agreement in the NCD responses concerning specific programs that are effective in reaching the "unchurched."[17] In a similar way, FACT research asked about the effectiveness of using a wide variety of outreach programs, including radio advertising, personal witness, revivals, and other evangelistic campaigns. Although each of these showed some modest impact, all of the evangelism programs showed a far greater correlation with membership vitality than with growth (Fig. 15). In short, the programs designed to recruit new members had more impact on those who implemented them than on their target populations.

Congregations grow when people care. One pastor said: "When

17. Survey Q-7 offers a dozen frequently used programs that show as many negative as positive correlations with growth, and none with compelling differences.

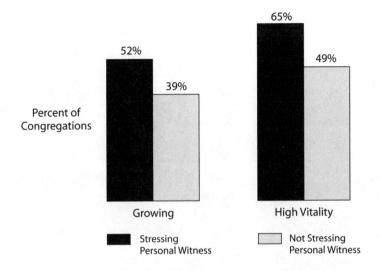

Figure 15. Personal Witness and Growing / Vitality

you're involved in listening to and mentoring couples, when you're involved in these family issues, all of a sudden your church becomes known as a community that cares. A divorce care group and those kinds of issues — you don't have to do the program kind of thing any longer" (FG 87-89). In essence, growing churches are upbeat: they are marked by positive expectations for the future. They cultivate an inviting atmosphere in worship, and they create imaginative activities that respond to the needs of members and visitors alike.

Inspiring and Relevant Worship Accompanies Growth

O. Generations Reflect Real Differences

The NCD research placed high emphasis on the work of clergy to bring individuals into a new relationship with Jesus Christ.[18] In the FACT

18. Survey Q-2: 58 percent of pastors in the largest and growing congregations say that in the last three months they have personally assisted someone "in making a first-

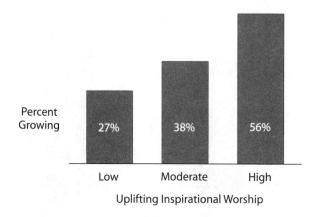

Percent Growing

| 27% | 38% | 56% |

Low　　　Moderate　　　High

Uplifting Inspirational Worship

Figure 16. Uplifting, Inspirational Worship and Growth

data, perhaps because the focus was more on congregational life, we see the importance of gatherings in faith. Together, the congregation has a relationship to God's presence in worship. Growing congregations, ones that are increasing in membership size, are significantly more likely to rate their worship as "uplifting" and "inspirational" (Fig. 16). These responders do not report that their worship was flawless, nor were they unwilling to change it. Rather, they seemed to reclaim the notion that "public worship" was a witness to their faith and thus a time of outreach and evangelism. In this way growing churches shared with others their collective awareness of the power of God in their lives through a wide variety of inclusive, invitational worship events.

The essential nature of preaching and the sacraments celebrated in Christian churches is an invitation to new life and transformation, and thus the call to begin or renew this life is always present. When a congregation is especially conscious of its missionary calling, it will examine its language, its music, its communication style, and its use of

time affirmation of faith in Jesus Christ as Lord and Savior," compared to 42 percent of pastors in smaller churches. Survey Q-26: 23 percent of pastors in the larger churches say they have assisted more than 20 people to first-time commitments in the last six months, compared to 4 percent of the smaller churches. At the same time, there is virtually no difference in the amount of time reported to be spent in sermon preparation and teaching or leading Bible study (Survey Q-30a, Q-30b).

the arts from the point of view of "seekers" and their generation, who have come in search of something ultimate. Whether a church is "seeker-driven" or "seeker-friendly,"[19] as are many congregations across the country, it is intentional about the impact of worship on the different generations that attend (see Chapter One of the present volume for a more complete examination of mission history and practice). One pastor in the study worked on "informal worship that had great substance but also engaged people, and was far more visual, far more experiential. Let them pray, let them see. Show a video from *The Lion King*, pick the treatment and drive it home. Worship is key" (FG 97-00).

P. Make Innovation Relevant

Adaptive change in worship characterizes rapidly growing churches, particularly among various streams of the Protestant tradition. One pastor caught the spirit: "Our worship style has changed so that I had to be willing to adapt to the change. To give up on what I believed or enjoyed and recognize somewhat — that's what I was learning while adapting" (FG 87-89). One measure of adapting in worship is the willingness by leaders to incorporate a contemporary instrument, such as an electronic keyboard, into their musical program. Responses in the FACT data are dramatic when the rate of growth is correlated with the frequency of electronic instrument use as a measure of innovation. These correlations can be seen throughout all Protestant groups — liberal, moderate, and evangelical (Fig. 17). Yet many pastors and other leaders have been surprised by the depth of emotional resistance caused by even minor changes in the worship service, sometimes known as the "worship wars." One strategy in response has been to conduct worship in two or more styles at different times during the weekend, one traditional while others are more seeker-oriented or contemporary. Despite efforts at blended worship, no combination pleases everyone. But innovative congregations communicate the willingness to accommodate to different tastes in music — and also with liturgical dance, drama, and multimedia resources.

---

19. Using language developed by Willow Creek Community Church in Barrington, IL.

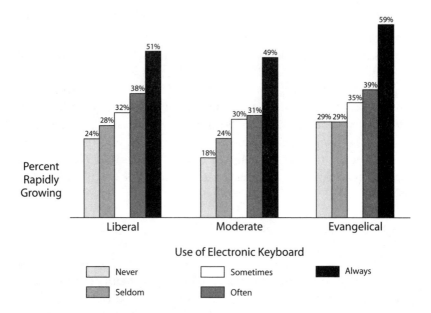

Figure 17. Liberal / Moderate / Evangelical and Electronic Keyboard

Flexibility: Fixed Plans Must Bend or Break

Q. Use Generational Differences Creatively

Through the window of worship we see ample evidence of the NCD hypothesis that new-church clergy need "a genuine affinity for local culture and context." The FACT report suggests that new congregations, like children, are as much the product of their time as they are the result of their theological parents. They bear the imprint of the culture and context from the generation in which they were born. These changing patterns (Fig. 18) show the shift in elements of worship based on the dates of congregational formation. Similar shifts can be seen in leaders' decisions to use piano and organ, for example, compared with the use of the electric guitar and drums, or other percussion instruments (see the FACT report for an extended discussion). Beyond the particular elements of worship, these figures dramatize how successful congregations speak the language of the community they are seeking to reach.

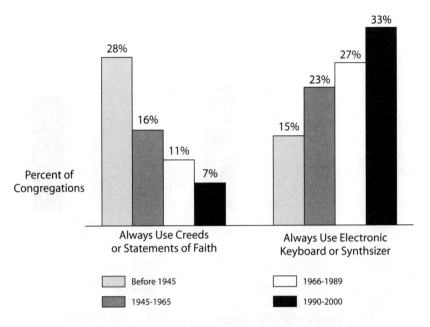

Figure 18. Use of Creeds / Keyboard and Founding Date

The NCD data show, surprisingly perhaps, that pastors of the larger and growing churches were unlikely to have had experience as youth pastors.[20] At the same time, they were more likely to adapt the worship service to reach people who were not active in church.[21] Apparently, because they place a high priority on reaching beyond custom and tradition, they seem more willing to engage in innovative worship. One church advertises worship around tables, as in a coffee shop, with the preacher stopping in the message to give participants an opportunity for questions and discussion. An older generation might find this awkward for worship, but those who frequent coffee houses may be

20. Survey Q-21e: 89 percent of the pastors in the largest and growing congregations had no experience as youth pastors, compared to 66 percent of pastors in smaller congregations.

21. Survey Q-31a: 39 percent of the pastors in the largest and growing congregations reported that in the first two years their worship experience was focused on reaching those not active in church, compared to 24 percent of pastors in smaller congregations.

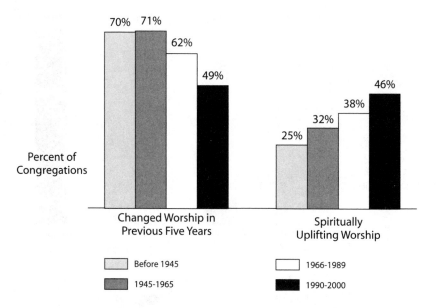

**Figure 19. Worship Change / Uplifting Worship and
Date of Founding**

more attracted to this approach. If, in addition, the message speaks
their language, the music is appealing, and the pace is right, then a
younger generation may find its way to church again.

R. Older Churches Must Change

With data from congregations organized decades earlier and reaching
back into a previous era, FACT confirms that change is essential over
time. Vision and planning that spoke to one generation must be adapted
to reach a new generation. In the FACT data, leaders of older congregations are less likely to report that their worship is spiritually uplifting
and more likely to have changed their worship in the past five years.
Many older churches see the need for change and respond (Fig. 19).

Change makes a difference. Church leaders who have accomplished significant change are likely to rate their worship as more spiri-

tually uplifting and inspirational. Vision must adapt to accommodate changes in the culture and context.

New-church starts are blessed with the freedom to choose their patterns of worship and congregational life — within the limits of the congregational culture they are trying to reach. As congregations grow older, they will need to change to keep in touch with younger age groups and with changing community populations. New churches must have plans, but planning should not obscure the need to remain flexible.

Typically, successful NCD pastors resist old patterns:

> Get rid of methods and models because part of the thing about experimentation and risk is that every church is a unique animal. The Spirit is going to make something different in every place. The models don't work. (FG 97-00)

S. Make Conflict Work for You

Change can be more attractive if it is easy and obvious; but often it is a painful and uncertain process. Again in the FACT data, worship provides a window for a larger experience that challenges new-church pastors. At bottom, with change comes conflict, and the more change is introduced, the more conflict results (Fig. 20). In some congregations, conflict seems to come with the territory. A veteran church organizer says:

> It's always hard for me to define what conflict is. There are certain churches where it seems like they're in conflict all the time. To me, that means either conflict is encouraged or promoted in such a way that it eventually happens. (FG 87-89)

Pastors describe how constructive use of conflict is essential to congregational growth and maturity; but they were still often caught off-guard by conflicts when they occurred.

Some leaders suggest that the living and adapting church must accept conflict as a way of life and learn constantly to deal with it in terms of the vision and mission of the church. Such leaders learn that conflict can help sharpen a church's vision and allow it to make essential changes. These are pastors who are particularly adept at training la-

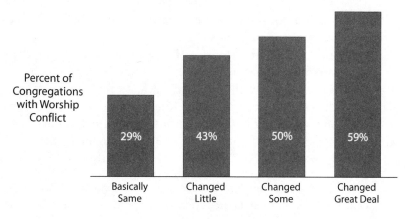

Figure 20. Changing Worship and Congregational Conflict

ity to develop basic leadership skills of conflict resolution, outreach, practical evangelism, and congregational planning.[22] From this range of responses, lay leaders were not just reducing conflict but converting energy toward common goals. Adversity becomes a friend over time, as one seasoned pastor reported: "After sixteen years, I think one of the things that I've tried to learn to do is to be positively transformed by adversity — to grow with the job, so to speak" (FG 90-93).

Education: Leadership Is Caught, Not Taught

T. We Cannot Teach Charisma

Effective new-church pastors have charisma, a powerful gift of the Spirit that seems to defy traditional programs for theological educa-

22. Survey Q-29: Pastors in the largest and growing congregations report training the original lay leaders — as compared to smaller congregations — ("some" and "a great deal") in conflict resolution (31 percent vs. 14 percent), outreach programs (61 percent vs. 42 percent), practical evangelism (50 percent vs. 31 percent), congregational planning (65 percent vs. 31 percent), etc.

tion. Confounding expectations, the FACT data clearly suggest that the more education church leaders received, the more they were aware of their own inadequacies (Fig. 21). New-church-development pastors, while exhibiting the same sort of "charisma," tend to seek advice from other pastors, thus balancing training and experience as input for ministry.[23] Training clergy for such pioneering leadership may require unique forms of one-on-one mentoring and spiritual formation that run counter to seminaries as educational institutions. NCD pastors need a kind of radical innovation that can function comfortably without conventional systems of institutional support. As numerous focus-group members said in a variety of ways, "Seminaries are not preparing men and women to be evangelists and developers" (FG 90-93).

This research raises significant questions about the capacity of existing church structures in seminaries and denominational offices to identify, train, and support the autonomous and sometimes anti-institutional character of effective new-church pastors. Every living institution faces challenges to develop innovative leaders who break conventional norms to renew and strengthen their foundations. This may require new forms of peer education in places and ways chosen by the new-church developer. NCD data, though not exactly supporting any specific path of choosing and training successful NCD pastors, invite wide experimentation in peer support, boot camps, monthly networking, and on-the-job sourcing. Nothing works for everyone, but entrepreneurial innovators seem to find what they need when they need it.

U. Creative Leaders Can Be Nurtured

Denominations that support innovative peer training and equipping systems invest considerable resources in making sure that — regardless of prior academic training — church planters are prepared to do the entrepreneurial work of beginning something from scratch and building it into a faith-based, spirit-filled community. Such high-risk invest-

23. Although the NCD survey was designed to uncover the essential educational programs to generate highly productive church leaders (cf. Survey Q-12-16, *passim*), it showed remarkable similarities to the FACT data in their mutual failure to identify effective educational programs and strategies.

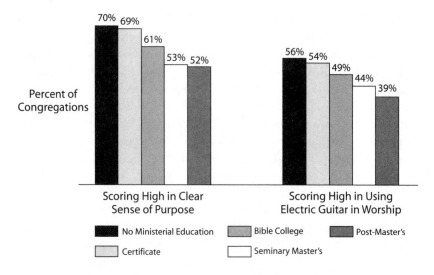

Figure 21. Clear Purpose / Electric Guitar and Education

ment in NCD leadership can be measured, not by testing the skills of the student, but by results in the field of practical application. Effective pastors are known by the energy their leadership generates in the congregations they serve. In FACT, they are seen in the way that congregations share their sense of purpose and mission, and the members believe that they are organized to achieve those ends (Fig. 22).

New-church developers tend to be entrepreneurial, loosely attached to their denominations, driven by a desire to create something new and better, and willing to seek help when and where they need it.[24] Every pastor's journey is unique, but the following quote catches the spirit of many:

> I began as a chemical engineer in college, and I've had interest in a variety of things. I've picked up some pastoral skills and counseling skills along the way, so there are multiple places where I think I can

24. Survey Q-36a: 41 percent of pastors in the largest and growing congregations report that they frequently ask advice of more experienced pastors, significantly more than pastors in all other congregations.

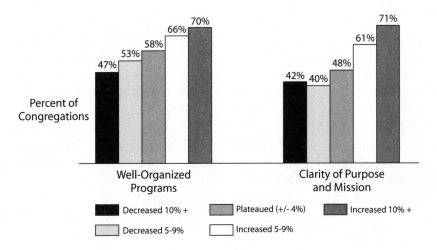

Figure 22. Well-Organized / Clarity and Growing Congregations

make some contact and interaction. I have a sense of relationship with people in a variety of arenas, and I think that's important and helpful as we begin to meet all of these new folk wherever they are. (FG 94-96)

Whatever their past, the "called" will carve out their own future.

Summary

Taken together, the FACT and NCD studies are remarkably coherent in several significant areas. "Location," when defined as an intentional focus on a particular population (or combination of population groups), is foundational to growth. A shared sense of vision gives a congregation energy and unity, but personal relationships are equally important to sustain vital congregations. The number of people who attend the organizing meeting of the congregation proves significant, but congregations gain momentum when the elements of worship are satisfying to old members while attracting new. Whatever strategies are initially successful, tenacity and flexibility are midwives to membership growth.

One final word on leadership, since it was the initial focus for the NCD study. In all we have seen, successful new-church pastors display an entrepreneurial style that remains more art than science, more chemistry than classroom, more Holy Spirit than denominational sanction. We have identified a number of elements that are statistically associated with church growth. In the final analysis, these data should humble those who would be managers among us. They affirm a more mystical Christian call that is validated, over time, only by the harvest. Not by educational degrees or specialized programs — but by their fruits you will know them.

Chapter Five

Guiding Insights
from the Research Project

H. STANLEY WOOD

What insights emerge from the analysis of the research survey? The survey queried over 700 founding pastors who had served in new congregations during the last twenty years of the twentieth century, representing the seven denominations participating in this study. This chapter will detail three major categories of discovery: first, the ways in which founding pastors of NCDs establish and practice their vision for congregational development; second, the support these founding developers had in initiating new congregations; and third, the process for selection of new-church-development pastors.

Robust findings emerged when we sorted the survey data by church membership size and worship attendance.[1] Understanding congregational dynamics by the number of worshipers on a typical Sunday (not Easter, Christmas, or holiday seasons) is a heuristic developed by Schaller, Rothauge, and Oswald. Their church typologies address the differing ways a church orders its life, its pastoral expectations, and its organization. Their conclusion is that churches of similar size have more in

---

1. The study used both worship attendance and membership size in order to include all seven denominations, since only four of the seven had worship attendance records. In NCD ministry, unlike traditional existing congregations, the membership size often lags behind the larger worship attendance in the initial years of development. Only rarely does this trend of more people in worship than membership enrollment continue in the life cycle of long-established congregations.

common with each other, despite denominational differences, than do churches of widely different size (even within the same denomination).

Using a new-church-development adaptation of "church types," we scrutinized the data with regard to the following categories:

- Family churches — fewer than 100 members, or fewer than 75 in attendance
- Smaller pastoral churches — 101 to 169 members, or 76-125 attendees
- Larger pastoral churches — 170-304 members, or 126-225 attendees
- Program churches — 305-540 members, or 226-400 attendees
- Corporate churches — 541 or more members, or 401 or more attendees[2]

The Establishment and Practice of Vision-Casting

In order to ascertain the NCD pastors' understanding and execution of vision, questions in the survey centered on:

- Aspects of a "vision for ministry"
- Any programs that might support such a vision
- Lay leadership in the NCD specifically empowered to share the vision of the faith community

Surveys have biases and assumptions embedded in them.[3] This survey asked missional theology questions about the practice of evan-

2. For a detailed explanation of "church types," initially adapted from Arlin Rothauge, *Sizing Up a Congregation for New Member Ministry* (New York: Seabury Press, undated), see also H. Stanley Wood, *NCD Guide, Stage II* (Vital Church Press, 2005), pp. 13-21. The study tabulated 704 surveys: "family type" churches totaled 186; smaller "pastoral type" churches totaled 178; larger "pastoral type" churches totaled 198; "program type" churches totaled 114; and "corporate type" churches totaled 28. In the latter two categories, three denominations represented the vast majority of these churches, namely, the ELCA, LCMS, and the PC(USA). The CRC and UCC have a few in these two largest church types; the other denominations had either an occasional one or no "program" or "corporate" NCDs. Various denomination offices conducted survey collection, and Dr. Keith Wulff in the Office of Research of the PC(USA) compiled the composite results.

3. Research Hypothesis H2 ("Effective NCD Clergy") exhibits a set of competen-

gelizing and how evangelism was understood. The survey probed into the contemporary practices of the original apostolic mandate to "make disciples," which launched a church-development vision fueled by Pentecost. Lesslie Newbigin writes of this apostolic vision: "Anyone who knows Jesus Christ as his Lord and Saviour must desire ardently that others should share that knowledge and must rejoice when the number of those who do is multiplied. Where this desire and this rejoicing are absent, we must ask whether something is not wrong at the very center of the church life."[4]

What distinctive beliefs and ministry practices characterized the actions of founding pastors from smaller to larger membership churches? From the inception of the new congregation's first public worship service, larger-membership pastors indicated that they were more likely to clearly articulate a "vision" for their new church, giving "evangelism" a "very high priority" in that vision.[5] This propensity of the larger-membership developers toward evangelization was given particular em-

---

cies and behaviors that cross denominational/ethnic boundaries: 2a) clergy who are able to articulate a compelling vision for ministry in NCDs are more likely to develop an effective (meaning "larger-membership") new start; 2b) clergy who exhibit key leadership qualities (to "give away" ministry to laity) and emphasize relational incorporation into the NCD fellowship; H3: NCD clergy who define evangelism holistically are more likely to develop effective new starts; 3a) clergy who focus on bringing people into a personal relationship with Jesus Christ are more likely to develop an effective new start; 3b) clergy who received formative training in the theology/methods of evangelism are more likely to develop effective new starts than those who lack such training; 3c) clergy who effectively disciple new members from converts to ministry participants are more likely to develop an effective new start. Survey Q-40d asked about the leadership priority of "clearly articulating a vision for the congregation." The top founders placed "vision-casting" (Wood profile point 3; also one of Hoyt's "marks of effective ministry") as a "very high priority." Top developers' answers to Survey Q-26 and Q-30 on evangelism strongly correlate with the hypothesis 3 evangelism emphasis in NCD start-up.

4. Lesslie Newbigin, *The Open Secret: Sketches for a Missionary Theology* (Grand Rapids: Eerdmans, 1978), p. 142.

5. Survey Q-40 asked for "the priority you gave to each of the following in providing leadership to this new-church start: Survey Q-40d, "clearly articulate a vision for the congregation"; Q-40f, "demonstrating leadership in evangelism." Seventy-one percent of the "corporate" church developers, compared to only 47 percent of the "family" church developers, gave "articulating a vision" a very high priority. In like manner, demonstrating leadership in evangelism was a "very high priority or high priority" for "corporate" church developers vs. "family" church pastors (46 percent vs. 32 percent).

phasis during the formative period of the first two years in the congregation. Larger-membership developers were the most likely to offer training in evangelism as a "very high priority" and to "empower others to lead." These developers tended not to center their leadership on their human limitations. They were the most likely to "strongly agree" on the importance for pastors "to identify, train, and empower lay leaders according to their gifts." The training began in a new-members class, where the pastor presented the congregational vision and direction 100 percent of the time in larger-membership NCDs. These pastors of larger churches were most likely to provide a new-members class that assigned a "new-member sponsor" to each new member and provided ministry deployment "very early" for ministry responsibilities.[6] They indicated that these members were a "major source" for contacting "unchurched prospects."[7] This means that these larger-membership developers sought the missional activity best embodied in the Incarnation, as Newbigin says:

> Jesus . . . did not write a book but formed a community. This community has at its heart the remembering and rehearsing of his words and deeds. Insofar as it is true to its calling, . . . [the community] becomes the place where men and women and children find that the gospel gives them the framework of understanding, the "lenses" through which they are able to understand and cope with the world.[8]

6. Survey Q-35 and Q-39c and d: "corporate" church developers scored the highest (by a 20 percent margin) for offering new-member classes where the congregational "vision and direction" were presented and sponsors were assigned. They also indicated that they were more likely to offer training in evangelism. In short, they empowered others to lead as their "very high priority." In answering Survey Q-36e, 70 percent of the larger-membership church developers "strongly agreed" to lay training, compared to 61 percent to 55 percent of the smaller-membership pastors. Survey Q-33, on assimilating new members, revealed that the majority of "corporate" church developers either "always" or "usually" assigned a new-member sponsor for each new member, compared to a 2-1 ratio over the smaller-membership NCD pastors; "corporate" church pastors practiced a "very early" recruitment of new members for ministry responsibilities and for involvement of new members in a small group.

7. Survey Q-31e asked whether "members were a major source for unchurched prospects." The "corporate" church pastors were twice as likely as "family" and "pastoral" church pastors to say that this "described exactly" what was happening in their NCD.

8. Lesslie Newbigin, *The Gospel in a Pluralist Society* (Grand Rapids: Eerdmans, 1989), p. 227.

During the formative stage of new-church development, the founding pastors of larger-membership churches were the most likely to have "numerous points of contact with the local community," which may help explain why their members were the primary or "major source for unchurched prospects." Furthermore, they reported greater attendance at the launch of their first public worship services. Once someone had come to worship in these larger-membership NCDs, the pastors showed a greater intent to "track visitors, contacts, and other prospects."[9] This discipline resulted in higher worship attendance by the third month (Q-4) after the first public worship service, as well as in the later stages of development.[10]

The survey explored whether or not denominational funding or site selections for the first worship service were associated with the size of the worshiping congregation that gathered at that time. Every NCD start-up received denominational funding; but it is interesting that this funding apparently had no correlation with eventual membership size. In terms of site selection, the data show that, regardless of the number of people at the first worship service, that first worship space tended to be leased or rented. Furthermore, the site tended to be a place that was well known in the community, such as a school or a movie theater.

In addition, the survey explored the methods pastors used to market the launch of public worship. For example, did these pastors use print media or radio ads? Which might be more effective? Surprisingly, this seemed to make little difference in the eventual size of the church. Similar kinds of publicity, meeting places, and frequency of in-

9. Survey Q-31 asked, "How well does each statement below describe your NCD experience in the first two years of public worship?" The section f statement read: "There was an intentional, systematic attempt to track visitors, contacts, and other prospects." The "corporate" church developers said this "describes exactly or well" their practice of ministry 100 percent of the time. Pastors of no other church "type" could say this as uniformly, and the smallest-church pastors indicated the least "intentional" or "systematic" follow-up practices.

10. Survey Q-4: nearly 50 percent of "corporate" church developers' congregations had 125 or more in their first public worship service, compared to only 13 percent in the smallest church "type." Survey Q-5: by the third month after public worship began, another third of the "corporate" churches were already showing public worship attendance of 90+, compared to fewer than 10 percent of the smallest church "type" at that attendance level.

formation meetings were used by all sizes of NCDs. The first worship sites of NCDs were almost uniformly selected after both "extensive demographic study" and "some preliminary local data gathering."[11]

As we have noted in Chapter Two, Lyle Schaller writes about population increases as a poor predictor of membership growth in NCDs. Given a fairly equal demographic starting line, the single most important factor determining which NCDs will develop a larger membership and which will remain small is what Schaller calls an "exceptionally competent minister."[12] Admittedly, competence has multiple facets and is found in diverse theological traditions. One missional assumption surrounding competence explored in this survey was how NCD leaders practice evangelism in their ministry context.[13] We asked participants to describe their invitational practices to outsiders. Specifically, we wanted to know whether newcomers were invited to experience the reign of God in a new faith community. Finally, we wanted to know what Newbigin describes as the "number of those" who professed for the first time — and/or reconfirmed after having been distanced from a faith community — that Jesus Christ is Lord and Savior.

We first asked how these founding pastors defined evangelism. The definition they chose most frequently was that evangelism means "proclaiming the gospel by calling people to repentance and personal faith in Jesus Christ as Lord and Savior and inviting them to member-

11. Survey Q-6 asked about the kind of place in which the first worship service was held; Survey Q-7, in its many subparts, asked about the kind of publicity and activities prior to the first worship that were used to invite first-time public worshipers. The survey answers revealed no major differences among NCDs of varying membership sizes or attendance. Survey Q-9, on site selection, confirmed that demographic studies and local data gathered were universally used for site selection for all NCDs surveyed, and hence the study of demographics could not, in and of itself, be considered a contributing factor to the membership or worship attendance size.

12. Lyle Schaller, 44 Questions for Church Planters (Nashville: Abingdon, 1991), p. 42.

13. "Evangelism would move from an act of recruiting or co-opting those outside the church to an invitation of companionship. . . . The community of the church would testify that they have heard the announcement that such a reign (the God who reigns in love and intends the good news for the whole earth) is coming and indeed is already breaking into the world. . . . To those invited, the church would offer itself to assist their entrance into the reign of God and to travel with them as co-pilgrims. Here lies a path for the renewal of the heart of the church and its evangelism." Darrell L. Guder, ed., *Missional Church: A Vision for the Sending of the Church in North America* (Grand Rapids: Eerdmans, 1998), p. 97.

ship in the church and service by deed in the world." The larger-membership pastors were only slightly more likely to choose this definition than those with smaller-membership NCDs. Furthermore, the religious backgrounds of all the pastors surveyed showed a great similarity of experience in evangelism. For almost all of them, evangelism had been emphasized in their home congregations. Larger-membership developers were more likely to come from childhood families that emphasized evangelism.[14]

Given the commonality in how they defined evangelism and the similarities of evangelism priorities in their home congregations, how did survey answers differ on the subject of evangelism practices? Despite similar beliefs about the importance and definition of evangelism, the survey revealed marked differences in the practices of evangelism. Assuming that time allocated indicated ministerial priorities, the study explored the ministers' use of time during the first twelve months. Larger-membership developers ranked highest in the priority they placed on time for evangelism: they tended to devote "a great deal of time to evangelism calling." They were also more likely to be participants in the Spirit's regenerative work in a person's making a first-time commitment to Christ as Savior and Lord. In fact, the evangelism practices of the larger-membership developers showed that they led all other NCD ministers in this particular kind of evangelism. Larger-membership pastors more frequently assisted in the making of a first-time faith commitment; indeed, many had assisted in such a commitment with twenty or more individuals in the previous six months. Larger-membership developers habitually practiced evangelization as a very high priority.[15]

---

14. Survey Q-23: smaller-membership developers chose this understanding of evangelism from 36 percent to 39 percent of the time, while the largest two church categories ranged from 44% to 44%. Survey Q-24a and b: only 35 percent of the smaller-church developers, compared to 59 percent of the larger-church developers, had a childhood evangelism emphasis.

15. Survey Q-25, 26 and 30: more than two thirds of the larger-church developers, during the first twelve months following the first worship service, indicated that they placed a "a great deal" of time in "evangelism calling," compared to fewer than 50 percent of the smaller-church NCD ministers.

Support for Initiating Congregations

NCD pastors were also asked to rate the value of support they received from national staff, judicatory staff, and congregations. Overall, the support they received, regardless of the size of their congregations, was considered "valuable." The support of judicatory staff was rated highest, followed in descending levels of help received from congregations and national staff.[16]

The survey differentiated among facets of this support: it cited local congregations, other NCDs, local judicatory staff, national staff, and seminary staff. The particular period for support was limited to the first two years after public worship commenced because those first twenty-four months comprise a critical start-up period: that is when congregational life is being established and support systems are being configured within the emerging congregation. Survey questions probed the following areas of potential support: program ideas, mentoring/coaching, lay-leader training, clergy training, financial assistance, and planning services.

Financial support, of course, is important. Local churches, judicatories, and national offices received the highest marks for the help they gave NCDs in the area of "financial assistance." This survey finding is underscored in Robert Hoyt's discussion of "new church developers and their connection to middle judicatories and national denominations" (Addendum C). In short, all NCD pastors recognize the importance of the financial support they receive.[17]

Mentoring and coaching are also critical to success. Most of the

16. Survey Q-32a and b: All five church-size types indicated appreciation for support. They all gave the largest percentage ratings to the top two categories, which rated that support either "very valuable" or "somewhat valuable," and the smallest percentages to "not at all valuable" and "received no help." The cumulative percentages from these top two categories for "help received from the following sources" was: from 49 percent to 82 percent for judicatory staff help, with smallest-membership NCD pastors at 47 percent and largest-membership NCD pastors at 82 percent; from 49 percent to 72 percent for help received from congregations; and from 52 percent to 59 percent for help received from national staff.

17. Survey Q-12e: Of the percentages for the multiple facets of support, "financial assistance" support came out with the highest percentages and ranged over the 50+ percent mark for all NCD pastors in churches of every size. Financial support from other NCDs or from seminaries was marginal.

participating denominations did not have a formal coaching or mentoring program in the first decade of the study period. It is significant that approximately half of the NCD developers in all membership sizes credited coaching and mentoring help given by the governing body staff; they recognized local judicatory staff for providing more help than the national staff offered.[18] Most participating denominations now have an established coaching or mentoring assistance program as a part of their NCD support system. These programs began to emerge during the second decade of our study (the 1990s).

Program ideas, lay training, clergy training, and planning services provided little help: only marginal support came from local churches, other NCDs, or local or national staffs for those areas of NCD initiation. For mainline denominations, which take pride in connecting the forms of church polity, this marginal support for home missions in new-church development is telling. From one perspective, it points to a gap in the denominational networks; from another perspective, the NCD may be the harbinger of a more fundamental change. What these data may show is not a gap in networking but a gap in time, a lag. Is new-church development such a different form of church development that existing church support and training systems are irrelevant or perhaps unusable by a form of church leadership that is inventing new modes of outreach? In this area, the survey leaves more questions unanswered than answered. Are existing support systems serving to maintain an aging Christendom church (as Darrell Guder suggests)? What would cutting-edge support systems for NCDs look like? Where can NCDs seeking appropriate support gain insights into programs, training, and planning?[19] The extended bibliography and websites at the end of this book suggest some possibilities.

Question 16 asked about the help that was offered to new churches by seminary staff. The results here are not overwhelming: NCD pastors'

18. Survey Q-14 and 15b: NCD pastors (from all church types) said they received more coaching and mentoring assistance from local judicatory staff (51 percent) than from national staff (36 percent).

19. Focus-group conversations document that the top developers sought out and adapted missionally focused assistance in such areas as worship, evangelism, and "discipleship-" vs. "membership-" based communities of faith (see Dudley's comparison with the FACT study results and Wood's profile traits under "faith-sharing" and "worship leadership").

acknowledgment of seminary support barely rose above single-digit figures.[20] On a positive note, it can be said that seminary staff offer "help" or give support in advance of a minister's call to the NCD frontier. Is it appropriate to anticipate that such support (embedded within a formal structure) would continue after placement in a ministry context? Perhaps more difficult to reconcile with these dismal numbers is the fact that every denomination represented maintains seminaries with continuing education programs. This, it would seem, might signal a clarion call to seminaries and the denominations that support them to include NCD support in their venues. Furthermore, in seminaries, including major nondenominational seminaries (which send large numbers of students for ordination in mainline denominations), the need for academically staffed positions in new-church development is obvious.[21]

There seems to exist a strong symbiotic relationship between an NCD congregation's focus on evangelism and its transformation from a maintenance to a missional *modus operandi*. Reclaiming the gospel from the cultural captivity of Christendom is challenging work: it is not easy to grapple with one's own cultural biases. It is clear that, despite their own cultural blinders, these NCD pastors energetically and prayerfully seek the formation of evangelizing communities. Evangelism — certainly as it has been understood and practiced by these NCDs — has rarely been part of the core curriculum within most seminaries. Nonetheless, these NCDs provide a unique incubator for the

20. Survey Q-16: Affirmative answers acknowledging seminary staff "help to NCDs" with program ideas, mentoring/coaching, lay training, clergy training, financial assistance, and planning services ranged from 0 percent to a high of 14 percent, with all single-digit percentages of "yes" answers being a high of 4 percent, and most of them being less.

21. Survey Q-16d asked about clergy training. From 0 percent to 3 percent of the NCD pastors acknowledged the clergy training they received from seminary staff as helpful, which means that 97 percent to 100 percent, depending on the church type of the NCD pastor responding, said they received "no" help for their NCD ministry from seminary staff. Only one of the participating denominations has a major degree and program specialization in new-church development, and this program was initiated at the end of the period covered by this study. (See Columbia Theological Seminary's website, www.CTSnet.edu, for "Advanced Degrees and Life Long Learning in New Church Development." In addition, Duke Divinity School has regularly offered summer continuing education courses in NCD, and Fuller Theological Seminary has frequent Doctor of Ministry classes in NCD.)

discovery of cutting-edge mission strategies. For one thing, an NCD, which is only a small boat in a denominational ocean, can turn quickly in the water. What doesn't work (or doesn't produce the depth and commitment desired) can be trimmed, tossed, or retooled. Seminaries that study these strategies can create innovative laboratories for missiology. The first priority of missiology is to bring *missio Dei* (as it is practiced and refined in current ministry contexts) into the center of seminary study. This has a strong supporting argument. "Mission," as Darrell Guder quotes Martin Kähler, "is the mother of theology."[22]

Support in planning for the area selected for a potential NCD site was available but bore little relationship to the eventual size of the NCD. Most of the time, the selection was done by a judicatory executive or a committee of the judicatory. Answers to site-selection questions indicated little differentiation in whether the NCD planted on a particular site became a smaller-, medium-, or larger-sized NCD. Only a quarter of the pastors surveyed indicated that a community canvass or survey led to site selection. On average, slightly under half of NCD pastors noted that sites were selected because of requests from local residents within their respective denominations.[23]

Site selection, nevertheless, is an important point. The results indicate that, though denominations may expend scarce resources to place and build an NCD, fewer than one-third of these churches will grow beyond roughly 500 members. Methods of site selection (as well as pastor recruitment and placement strategies) need extensive re-examination. For example, one denominational strategy might be to withhold funding for a site purchase until the NCD has established a multiple-year track record. Organizational maturity might provide a good benchmark for the creation of building blueprints.

22. See Chapter One of present volume, note 11.
23. Survey Q-9 asked about NCD site selection. Combining the top two options where checks were made on all answers that apply, the answers of "extensive demographic study" and "some preliminary local data gathering" were cited by NCD developers about 50 percent of the time. Sites chosen, in part, through "requests or inquiries from local residents of our denomination" ranged from 50 percent to a low of 40 percent; those selected by means of "community canvass or survey" ranged from 38 percent to 22 percent. Survey Q-10 asked who selected the site: nearly half the time this was done by a denomination executive or NCD committee, followed by a second method, a group of local church leaders or pastors (less than a third of the time).

Selection of NCD Pastors

Many of the participating denominations had begun some kind of selection or screening process for NCD clergy by mid-1995. The high financial commitments made by denominations in an effort to plant
NCDs, coupled with screening and selection processes employed at
that time, indicated that there were gaps in the correlation between denominational support and the projections of NCD potential. In other
words, in areas where some denominations expected NCDs to thrive,
many new churches stalled at smaller congregational levels in the
midst of large unchurched demographics. This gap led to a research
question that addressed the "assignment process" and the impact of
that process on eventual clergy effectiveness, as measured by the ratio
of the unchurched demographics to the worship size of the NCD. The
survey instrument thus addressed the NCD pastors' perception of this
selection process.[24]

The results are telling. One-third of the developers had volunteered to become NCD pastors. Nearly 50 percent said that a judicatory
or denominational staff member had recruited them.[25] Furthermore,
the survey queried these NCD pastors about whether the selection process involved formal assessments or screening prior to their placement.
The expectation was that denominational selection processes already
in place were contributing to "effective NCD pastor" selections. Over
700 NCD responding clergy said that about half of the time some kind
of formal assessment had influenced their being selected.[26] During the
latter half of the study period (about 1990 to 2000), most denomina-

24. Research Hypothesis 1b: The assignment process impacts the eventual success
of NCD clergy. Only in the 1990s did the ELCA and, to a lesser degree, the PC(USA) have
some verifiable evidence that this was the case from denominational sorting of larger-
membership NCD clergy answers. For the most part, this hypothesis was not affirmed
by survey results.

25. Survey Q-17 asked NCD clergy to select "all that apply"; in so doing, from 31
percent to 39 percent said they volunteered for NCD pastoral ministry, while the same
group of pastors said that a judicatory or denominational leader recruited them (from
46 percent to 55 percent).

26. Survey Q-18: The answers to whether or not a formal selection process was
used prior to clergy placement in the new-church start were split almost 50-50 between
yes and no answers, and answers categorized by church type revealed no particular pref-
erence for ability to choose either smaller-, medium-, or larger-church pastors.

tions had formalized selection mechanisms; prior to that time, informal but nonetheless influential selection processes had been at work for many years. Of course, these results raise questions about whether any formal (or informal) system is achieving the goal of matching qualified candidates with appropriate ministries. The results of this study suggest that the matching processes currently in place do not always identify effective leaders. Again, "effective" — in this narrow definition — means whether these denominations were able to choose pastors who had the skills to initiate and sustain growing communities of faith composed of formerly unchurched people.

The study asked about placement in the selection process: how were NCD clergy placed in a particular NCD call? The predominant modes of placement were either the normal processes used in the respective denominations or targeted placement by judicatory staff.[27] Again, the assignment process as it currently functions does not predict the future membership size of an NCD. Answers to this question were evenly spread across the varying membership/worship size of NCD congregations.

What efforts were made to "match" prospective NCD pastors' "gifts, strengths, and/or leadership style" to a prospective NCD ministry context?[28] The study asked the pastors to make only one response; by combining two of the response lines, the study captured nearly all of the respondents. As a group, they were selected by "a fairly thorough, though informal, matching process" and "some discussion of this topic occurred."[29] The results revealed no difference for the various sizes of NCD congregations, and this again calls into question the matching process. Almost all of the NCD clergy were placed by their denomination with an expectation of a larger-membership church.

27. Survey Q-19: Answers revealed that between 33 percent and 45 percent of NCD clergy were placed by "normal procedures used in" their respective denominations, and that, concurrent with this method of placement, many also answered that they were "specifically recruited for this new start by denomination or judicatory staff" (between 35 percent and 45 percent).
28. Survey Q-20.
29. Survey Q-20: Selections for an "informal matching process" were rated from 28 percent to 43 percent, and selections for "discussion of the topic occurred" were rated from 23 percent to 27 percent. Although answers to other options occasionally crept over single digits, no other selections received percentages comparable to the above.

Did these NCD developers have ministry experience as NCD pastors before assuming another NCD call? Had a significant number been senior pastors in established congregations before taking the NCD call? How could this knowledge be useful? There was a tacit assumption in nearly all the participating denominations that NCDs, which were usually planted in large population concentrations, would become larger-membership churches and thus become multiple-staff ministries. Hence the survey was designed to measure whether a pastor having prior NCD experience or having prior experience as a senior pastor in a larger-membership church could effectively start a larger-membership NCD. If so, this might be a useful marker for NCD pastor selection. But those surveyed revealed that few of them had had prior experience in planting a church; furthermore, their experience seemed to be a poor predictor of future congregational size. This also held true for those who had had senior pastor experience. We discovered, therefore, that prior NCD experience or senior pastor experience was not a reliable predictor of clergy effectiveness as measured by congregational size.[30]

The same question continued in another subpart: it asked respondents to list the number of years of service they had in various kinds of pastoral calls in established congregations prior to their NCD start. Such calls included service as a solo pastor, as an assistant or associate pastor in a multiple-staff church, or as a youth minister (ordained or lay). Regardless of the membership/worship size, more than 50 percent of the pastors in each size category had had more than five years of prior pasto-

---

30. Survey Q-21a and b: Part "a" asked pastors about the number of years of experience they had in NCD ministry prior to their present call. Most did not have any NCD ministry experience. Their responses were evenly spread among the church types, ranging from 66 percent to 80 percent. A second part of the "a" question asked those who had NCD experience prior to their present NCD call, how many years of NCD experience they had. The answers showed that the average number of years in NCD experience was 5-9; but this represented only a modest number of those surveyed. The percent spread over the queried pastors of all the church sizes was 10 percent to 18 percent. Part "b" asked about whether they had been senior pastors in established congregations. Depending on the church size "type," from 57 percent to 75 percent had not served as senior pastors prior to their NCD call; and of those who had served in this capacity, the largest percentage had been senior ministers for more than ten years. Once again, responses were evenly spread across smaller- to larger-membership churches (ranging from 18 percent to 21 percent). Only 11 percent of the NCD pastors serving "family" size NCDs had served as senior pastors for ten or more years.

ral experience.[31] But it's true that some denominations have an unwritten rule that NCD pastors must have had five or more years' pastoral experience before they will be considered for a NCD position. It is interesting to note that more than 25 percent of all founding pastors surveyed had no solo pastor experience (though they may have had other kinds of ministry experience). Among the leaders in the largest-membership NCDs, those without solo experience jumped to 39 percent. The same question investigated assistant or associate pastor ministry in a multiple-staff church: respondents either had no experience or only one or two years of multiple-staff pastoral experience.[32] The study made a final query about ministry experience in either lay or clergy youth ministry, and this question yielded greater diversity among NCD pastors: excluding large-membership pastors, an average of 72 percent had had no youth ministry experience. Of those who led large-membership NCDs, 89 percent had had no youth ministry experience, as Dudley notes in his chapter. Those ministers with extensive youth ministry backgrounds (6 percent of the large-membership pastors) had had ten or more years' youth ministry experience.[33] No leaders of congregations in other size groups approached that figure. Thus, youth ministry experience cannot be used as a predictor of future NCD membership size.

Some Concluding Thoughts

This survey provides a valuable snapshot of NCD life and thought. Using responses from over 700 NCD clergy, the data show a bright pic-

31. Survey Q-21c: The percentages for combining two periods (5-9 or 10 or more years) of service as a "solo pastor in an established congregation," among all church size classifications, varied from a low of 52 percent to a high of 60 percent.

32. Survey Q-21d: The percentages for combining two periods (none or 1-2 years) of service as "an assistant or associate pastor in a multiple-staff church," among all church size classifications, varied from a low of 44 percent for "family" church pastors to a high of 58 percent for "program" church pastors.

33. Survey Q-21e: The percentages of service as a "youth minister" of the pastors of the first four church-size classifications—moving up in size from "family" to "program" size—are respectively: 66 percent, 68 percent, 71 percent, 84 percent, which averages 72 percent with no youth ministry experience. Conversely, in the highest youth-ministry experience category of "ten or more" years' experience, the percentages, moving up in size from smallest church type to the largest ("corporate") type, are respectively: 2 percent, 5 percent, 5 percent, 0 percent, and 6 percent.

ture of pastors who are filled with the passion of gospel-sharing, who struggle with denominational constraints, and who labor with the Holy Spirit to create strong and viable communities of faith. By listening to them we can learn some useful lessons about visioning, about support, and about the processes of placement.

The questions concerning the establishment and practice of vision were somewhat vague by design. They could not probe the nuances of what constitutes a vision or how it might be carried out. (This was done in focus groups with a limited number of NCD developers.) Even after accumulating these data, we need to do more work here. Guder aptly captures the tension at work here as these pastors seek to create a vision shaped by an apostolic calling in the midst of denominations laden with the vestiges of Christendom. One aspect of the apostolic calling is faithful witness to sharing the gospel message. These pastors step into the flow of practical evangelism. They share the Good News, and they put in place follow-up structures that invite individuals into a missional community of faith. This study suggests that those pastors who are most obedient to issues of mission and community are those whose ministries grow to a far greater size relative to those of their less assiduous peers.

The significance of these findings speaks to denominational planning and selection protocols. Given an accurate demographic starting point of unchurched people in an area, denominational leaders can safely estimate the size of a possible NCD. One key factor in achieving size targets is related to a particular pastor's skill and practice of the apostolic call of the church. A candidate who is less skillful and whose practice is intermittent will reap a smaller harvest. Thus, in making decisions about sites for church planting, about candidate selection, and about potential growth indices, denominations can gain insight from this study into how missional leadership may affect ultimate growth. This is not to suggest that this work can or should be done apart from the leading of the Holy Spirit. It is the mystery of God's grace that leads individuals into life in Christ and into the life of the church. But pastors who learn and practice the skills of missional church-building seem to work most effectively in partnership with the Holy Spirit's healing of a fallen world.

Many pastors operate within a single paradigm of pastoral ministry. But there are marked differences in pastoral styles, and these styles seem remarkably similar within churches of similar size — regardless of whether the church is just beginning or is long established. It is safe to say that virtually all NCD pastors begin by working with people on a one-to-one basis or with a very small, tight-knit group. But over time, the pastors who continue in this style tend to create smaller churches. Pastors who shift from pastor-centered to lay-leader-centered pastoral care create the energy and momentum for larger churches. The pastor in a larger-membership church is likely to know and love the members of the church, but others carry on the pastoral care aspects of ministry within the congregation. This does not mean that there is a diminished sense of a caring church family in the larger churches; rather, pastoral care in larger-membership churches normally takes place in sub-congregational contexts, through programs, small groups, nurture groups, choirs, and the like. Ideally, larger churches intentionally build the nurture and care of each church member into the sub-congregational contexts of their vital, care-giving small groups. Clergy staff is available in a crisis, but in effective larger-attendance churches the clergy staff, as well as the lay staff, tends to train ongoing leaders for routine matters. They identify and empower laypeople who have the spiritual gifts of mercy and pastoring.

Therefore, though the survey findings did not probe the specifics of vision, some general indicators can be discerned. For example, there seem to be hints of a vision based on the number of people who attended the very first public worship service, which seems to be a key indicator of momentum: those with larger numbers at the first service developed into large churches, and those with smaller numbers were more likely to stay small. The how and why of this phenomenon provides interesting starting points for future research. The phenomenon seems tied to both the style traits of the developer (see Hoyt and Wood) and to the relevance of the gospel message (see Guder). The NCD survey seems to indicate that, despite the fluidity of leadership styles and skills in a shifting and growing congregation, one steadfast role the larger-membership pastor retains is that of evangelist-in-residence. Furthermore, the pastor continually empowers and equips others to create a growing faith community by experiencing the passion of faithful witness.[34]

34. I have put it this way in the *NCD Guide, Stage II*, p. 14: "When a particular program reaches the participation size that can no longer incorporate any more people,

The role of the seminary is crucial to the support and development of these pastors. Seminaries that take up the challenges of crafting a theologically driven vision, of teaching skills in missional leadership, and of providing personal support for those interested in pursuing the NCD have established an agenda for the seminary curriculum and continuing education that is relevant for those on the cutting edge in the twenty-first century. Seminaries willing to abandon more fully the vestigial ideas of Christendom (which leans toward creating clergy maintainers of the status quo) will discover new venues for creativity and innovation. Training attentive to the paradigms of new and revived churches might focus on effective ways to lead and empower laity for ministry and might explore ways of inviting people outside the church to experience the mystery of the sacred. Gathering a new congregation creates a laboratory for missiological education and needs the academy's theological critique. Perhaps the use of "case studies," in which seminary students are engaged with the theological implications of missional leadership, coupled with internships in which such leadership might be practiced, would be a good starting point. Karl Barth is helpful here. He defines the congregation as "the event which consists in gathering together *(congregation)* those men and women *(fidelium)* whom the living Lord Jesus Christ chooses and calls to be witnesses to the victory he has already won, and heralds of its future universal manifestation."[35] Developing leadership skills for missional witness can prepare twenty-first-century clergy for the next generation of NCDs and renewed congregational ministries.

---

then the organizing pastor and lay leaders develop a new program, and so on. A hallmark of effective NCD growth is that programs are *high-quality programs.* The ability to start successive, high-quality programs that minister to and incorporate the formerly unchurched is one of the differences between a maintenance/survival NCD and a growing NCD. Most new churches focusing on being Program-type Churches will start at least one new program that touches the felt and real needs of the unchurched persons in its ministry area every six months to a year. Most new churches starting with 100 to 200 in worship have a similarity with other smaller-membership churches in that they have limited human and financial resources and can only manage one or two main outreach programs at a given time. Therefore, initially, a new church needs to focus on doing one or two outreach programs well, and ideally these programs are relating the gospel in contextually relevant ways to the unchurched in the target population of the NCD ministry area."

35. Karl Barth, *Church Dogmatics* (Edinburgh: T. and T. Clark, 1962), Vol. IV, p. 72.

In addition to the work of the seminary, the denominations them-selves provide critical support for NCDs. Financial support from local churches, local judicatories, and national denominational offices scored four times higher than financial support from other NCDs.[36] Perhaps not surprisingly, the survey reveals that any financial gift from one NCD to another was rare. However, gifts of great worth do not al-ways come in the form of money. What might prove to be very helpful is a networking system between churches at different stages and genera-tions of congregational development. This networking might certainly include financial support; but it might also include mission trip ex-changes for special outreach programming, web connections, congrega-tional workdays, and a prayer network between congregations and clergy. In point of fact, this might be an effective model by which more-established NCDs could mentor congregations that are just beginning.

Currently, little coaching and mentoring occurs between NCDs and other local churches — or between NCDs themselves. At times, coaching and mentoring is provided by local judicatory and national of-fices.[37] More than half of the NCD pastors surveyed affirmed that they had received mentoring and coaching from the staff of a governing body. The survey did not address the various points in organizational life when coaching and mentoring might prove effective. This is a ques-tion for further study. Many of the participating denominations are for-malizing a coaching program. In one case, for example, the denomina-tion is pairing its most effective NCD pastors (who have at least seven years of experience) with new NCD pastors in the field; this connection is being made through an innovative partnership between the national NCD office and national grass-roots NCD pastor associations.

These data show that the best placement systems currently are in-adequate, at least if the goal of creating an NCD is to achieve the growth potentials indicated in demographic planning. Many unchurched people today live near once-viable NCDs that were costly financial and personal undertakings but failed to grow to their full potential. These churches

36. Survey Q-13e: Depending on the membership size of the congregation, be-tween 77 percent and 89 percent said that they did not include other NCDs in their be-nevolence giving.

37. Survey Q-12 and 13b: More than two-thirds of those surveyed said that mentoring and coaching from either other NCDs or local churches was not part of their experience.

failed to reach many of the unchurched. This is problematic for denominations, which have increasingly dwindling funds for the initiation of new churches. Given the limited financial resources to support an NCD start, the clear expectation that the new church will become a large-membership church shows a continuing need to rethink old assumptions of appointment and selection. This will not be an easy task in old, established denominations. Donald Miller, who investigated three of the fastest-growing NCD movements, known as Calvary, Vineyard, and Hope Chapel,[38] makes this point eloquently:

> Centralized bureaucracies value uniformity. They also build, almost by definition, a hierarchical organization structure with layers of managers and supervisors in between the constituency and the leader at the top. Managing this structure requires uniform policies and a regular flow of memorandums. Advancement in the organization often depends on seniority or accumulation of credentials, and leaders with new ideas are typically held in check because of the threat they pose to the prevailing organizational structure. By decentralizing authority, new paradigm churches (e.g., Hope Chapel) and movements circumvent this movement toward routinization. Governance is based on trust and personalized relationships rather than policies and procedures. And training occurs through mentored relationships rather than through formalized and centralized educational institutions.[39]

A way forward for new-church development in denominations that value the connecting tissue of their congregations and judicatory structures might be to aid existing churches to start new churches, in-

---

38. The steering committee of this project visited the parent congregation and founding pastor of Hope Chapel. In a lengthy interview with Ralph Moore and some of his staff, we explored their selection process for Hope Chapel NCD pastors. We found that they "grow their own leadership" through a rigorous period of mentorship, which involved incremental ministry responsibilities given to budding leaders. NCD pastors were "home grown" and commissioned to new starts by parent congregations. Hope Chapel has a high success rate of NCD pastor selection. Proven leaders are sent out with the DNA of the parent congregation, and the support and accountability of the NCD start-up are located regionally and locally through the sending congregations.

39. Donald E. Miller, *Reinventing American Protestantism: Christianity in the New Millennium* (Berkeley: University of California Press, 1997), p. 143.

cluding the sending of "home-grown" leadership to be NCD pastors. Seminary training could underscore and challenge what was being learned in a fluid and seamless transaction. What would happen if many more churches with a missional vision to extend the kingdom of God in a nearby place were empowered to extend their missional vision in church planting? How would denominations with long-established and centralized polity structures deal with this new paradigm approach to new-church development? Building relationships of trust among church leaders, denominational leaders, and seminary faculties is the first step. Miller suggests that "the organization genius of the founders of new paradigm movements is that they are willing to risk failure by giving autonomy to creative upstart leaders."[40]

Thus an amalgam of possibilities seems on the horizon. As leaders and led continue to carry the gospel message forward, exciting possibilities for church planting, visioning, support mechanisms, and placement protocols are yet to be discovered as we continue to explore how the Holy Spirit moves and creates the twenty-first-century church. The results of this survey give us clues to future direction, focus, and priority as we observe these "unadorned clay pot messengers" who are serving, in the power of God's Spirit, as extraordinary leaders for these extraordinary times.

40. Miller, *Reinventing American Protestantism*, p. 143.

Conclusion

This study represents the most complete exploration of the new-church development (NCD) phenomenon as it is currently understood within the United States. The study, though somewhat incomplete and flawed, provides more information about this important work than does any other study to date. To begin an NCD is challenging work — at times heartbreaking, frustrating, and painful. It can also be exhilarating, enjoyable, and deeply satisfying. The crucible of this labor is not for everyone, not even for everyone who might wish to try it. At its heart is the apostolic call of Christ. At its outcome is a living, breathing community of faith, rooted in the gospel call and reaching to extend that call outward in vibrant witness. Creating an effective NCD requires the prayer, thought, and muscle of a team of people at the denominational, local, and seminary levels. This team, once assembled, is really charged with two great tasks: first, they must find the right place; second, they must find the right person. This study has focused exclusively on the second task: how to identify, recruit, select, train, nurture, place, evaluate, and support these leaders. Most importantly, then, this study examines, for the first time, the components and behaviors of the new-church leaders across broad denominational boundaries. It presents a trans-ecclesiastical leadership profile that provides a foundation for studying these leaders and the work they do more closely than ever before.

It is important to remember that the success of these leaders must be viewed against a landscape of tremendous loss. Each of the seven denominations in this study is losing more members each year than it is gaining. Each denomination admits to having many established congregations in need of transformational leadership and redevelopment. And each denomination sees developing new churches as one of the bright hopes for the future. Nonetheless, many of the new churches planted by these denominations have produced only marginal results. This study suggests that a very specialized set of personality traits and behavioral characteristics in the NCD pastor himself or herself may be necessary for new-church growth. Training and placing clergy who lack these foundational personality and behavior traits may produce only a mediocre harvest at best.

The data from this study identify a unique group of profile traits that seem inherent to effectiveness. If this can be taken to mean that denominational executives and lay leaders should be actively calling and nurturing leaders who display these traits, then a compelling question arises: What percentage of currently ordained clergy or those in training to be ordained might display these characteristics? The view is muddy because larger systemic issues of Christendom cloud the lens. But one great truth seems to emerge clearly from the remnants of Christendom: the church has lost its missional focus. That focus needs to be restored. Churches are no longer evangelizing communities. Given the losses that these seven denominations continue to accumulate, the need to restore that focus becomes achingly apparent, and yet the barriers to restoring the focus seem particularly formidable.

If these effective NCD leaders, and others like them, are to be welcomed into positions of pivotal leadership, then denominations, seminaries, and other training institutions will have to be receptive to them. The solution to the staggering losses sustained by these seven denominations is not to be found in business as usual. It is not a remedy found in more judicatory planning, or in more new-church-growth programming, or even in a disembodied theory of applied evangelical theology. This research suggests that leaders who are trained to exercise these gifts and skills responsibly and maturely will thrive in new-church development. Those who are interested in the future of missional growth would benefit by nurturing those who display this combination of learned skills and special charisma.

All of these NCD pastors successfully navigated through the education and ordination requirements typical of Protestant denominations. With few variations, clergy in these denominations matriculate through undergraduate school, complete seminary training on the graduate level, and pass ordination examinations. Given the intensity, duration, and regimentation of these demands, it is amazing that leaders who possess the traits described in this study (which are so clearly connected to the growth of effective NCDs) ever clear the hurdles. The fact that they can clear the hurdle of denominational call is surprising. Perhaps it is not surprising that the ordination gauntlet is geared to produce pastors for existing churches, not for new churches. Many of the skills and behaviors found in these leaders, such as perseverance, risk-taking, adapting, and the organizational aspects of self-starting, are learnable skills. Granted, some of these traits are fired by raw charisma and are God-given; but even as such, they can be sublimated or cultivated.

This research is an impressive and helpful affirmation of the biblical patterns for congregational formation, as read and interpreted by the missional theologian. But certain flaws and limitations of the quantitative research methodology do emerge. Obviously, the work of the Holy Spirit cannot be quantified, and, with appropriate modesty, this study never makes that claim. That sense of awe at what God has done in so many of the new congregations surveyed gives ample evidence of this modesty as well. However, from the perspective of missional theology, there are questions to be raised about the governing assumptions of the study design. This leads, by implication, to questions concerning the general approach to the formation of new congregations, at least by the mainline denominations here represented.

The concerns emerge from the concepts articulated in Chapter One regarding the post-Christendom context of the church in North America today — and the continuing impact of that Christendom legacy. The research instrument itself, by immediately focusing on the process of the first public worship service, the activities that preceded it to draw together participants as potential founding members, and the various options for organizational and institutional development, creates the impression that it assumes the "maintenance of the already existing Christendom tradition" as the key purpose for a new-church development.

We should not overstate this: there is certainly evidence in some of the anecdotal reports of the focus groups of dissatisfaction with the assumptions of that legacy, dissatisfaction with the entrepreneurial conditioning of the church in our society, and especially dissatisfaction with the operative criteria for "success." It might be asking too much to expect critical confrontation with the profound shape of our post-Christendom context in the formulation of survey questions and the analysis of their results. The focus groups demonstrate that maintenance and mission are both present and in a healthy tension with one another. But the awareness of the challenge to the church today to become a missional movement within and often against our context is not documented. Perhaps this could emerge as a next stage of research. Such research might find ways to assess how the West's theological reductionism of both the gospel and the church's mission implicitly shapes the attitudes and assumptions that still guide denominational new-church development.

That these issues remain for the most part unquestioned and unexamined does not reduce the value of this study; rather, it is a compelling and instructive illustration of the difficulty inherent in the kind of "paradigm shift" in which we find ourselves as we move out of and beyond Christendom. The questions we ask control the answers we get. The research instrument asks about evangelism, about program development, about leadership styles, about denominational strategies and tactics — and it produces very useful insights. They are expanded on in the focus-group discussions, where there is evidence of a great deal of awareness of the larger theological issues, though not in ways that can be readily analyzed in a systematic way. Thus it appears that the Christendom mindset is subtly at work; this is in itself an important finding, but not surprising, and it demonstrates what we have observed to be true, at least within the mainline traditions, in other contexts. We have yet to learn how to ask questions that reveal a maintenance mindset or stimulate an exploration (or rediscovery) of the radically missional nature of the church. The survey regarded it statistically very important that the new church pastor should "listen to people and respond to their needs" (Survey Q-40a), "clearly articulate a vision for the congregation" (Q-40d), "develop goals and objectives" (Q-30e), and "demonstrate leadership in evangelism" (Q-30f). There is no further specification, theologically, about what the needs of the people might be, what a vision ought to be, or what the goals and objectives ought to be about. One could argue that such intentionality would not be appropriate in the kind of qualitative research conducted here. However, cultural assumptions are always being made, in ways obvious or subtle, when a study such as this frames its questions. A further discussion of these findings — and the new themes they generate — may find ways to probe these deep levels of "Christendom assumptions and attitudes."

To take one example, the priority assigned by the new-church pastor to "respond to current issues" (59 percent to 43 percent) ranks below "building self-esteem" (64 percent to 73 percent). Since neither "current issues" nor "self-esteem" is more precisely defined, one should be cautious about drawing conclusions. But these factors, and their interaction, could legitimately be interpreted as more evidence that the missional nature of the church in these new congregations is still understood more individualistically than corporately, more focused on salvation (however defined) than on world-oriented witness, and thus that the power of the Christendom mindset continues to be unchallenged and its assumptions unquestioned.

But one should not overemphasize these factors. One might well argue that an empirical methodology for assessing the radically missional character of the church in the aftermath of Christendom is yet to be developed. The issues are clearly very hard to reduce to simple categories and are not easily receptive to quantification. Thus it is a useful finding of this study that the church's confrontation with its gospel and ecclesial reductionism after Christendom is only in its beginning stages. Here is where much work remains to be done.

Another challenging question pointing toward future research is this: How might this study inform seminary education, supervised ministry, and professional recruitment? What would these training and placement venues look like if the gifts and skills revealed in this study were an integral part of ministry training for all clergy? What would they look like if qualifying for leadership meant showing the potential for building an evangelizing community of faith where large portions of the congregants were formerly unchurched? Placement in a ministry setting where ministry skills that are taught in the classroom can be practiced is not a new paradigm for theological education. Some form of this paradigm is behind the requirements for certain core courses of seminary curriculum, supervised ministry, and clinical pastoral education. This research forces us to ask whether this combination of critical profile traits is being "taught" in denominational seminaries or "caught" in supervised ministry assignments. In a church atmosphere where dynamic leadership might be rightfully questioned, might it also be valued as a gift of the Holy Spirit and nurtured by classroom learning and practice? This research raises questions about the appropriateness of our current paradigms for leadership preparation.

Since the training venues where missional church vision can be caught and taught are relatively few, it is possible that mainline denominations can learn from the experiential training increasingly used by nondenominational churches (see Chapter Five). Unencumbered by the bureaucratic processes attached to traditional Protestant clergy preparation, many large nondenominational churches have become, in effect, mini-seminaries (e.g., Hope Chapel, Vineyard, Calvary Chapel). These churches select, nurture, and train evangelizing witnesses — and they mentor them closely. Those who participate find a home of like minds. This is, sadly, not true of many of the mainline NCD pastors who participated in this study. Although not expressly discussed in this research, one clear inference we can draw from the interaction of these NCD pastors is that they form a distinctive breed. Despite denominational differences, many of these pastors had much more in common with each other than they did with traditional pastors from their own denominations. This research, then, raises questions about the formation of supportive faith communities for these NCD pastors, both within the seminary and beyond.

For too long a time, very little has been known about these NCD pastors, their work, and their working styles. This study provides an immense amount of information that yields practical value for those involved in the training, supervision, and support of these pioneers in ministry. Those who must staff NCD positions, for example, can use the constellation of leadership traits as a primer for constructing interview questions and establishing benchmarks of ministry experience. When we add this study's results to the results of the FACT study, we can set forth guidelines on how to select, develop, and hone candidates and church sites through the leading of the Spirit. Those in seminary education and training can certainly use this study as a starting point for shaping and creating ministry contexts and learning experiences that may be more consonant with the personalities, needs, and drives of unique NCD pastors-to-be. Work on all these dimensions of ministry preparation and placement is long overdue. It is our hope that this work will stimulate conversation and change in the churches in ways that will further God's kingdom.

Volume Two of this study details ethnic research among African-American, Hispanic, Asian, Korean, and Native American NCD pastors who are functioning within the mainline denominations that participated in this study. The study of racial-ethnic minorities will unearth new facets of the trans-ecclesiastical profile, new behaviors and skills, and new congregational paradigms that will further inform and shape our thinking.

DARRELL L. GUDER
H. STANLEY WOOD

Who These Extraordinary Leaders Are:
NCD Pastors' Responses

ROBERT S. HOYT

The twenty-four characteristics of effective mission developers listed in this discussion are not necessarily unique to mission developers, but they are common characteristics of these very effective developers. The success these leaders achieved was in reaching people who were previously without a church connection or were inactive members. As such, these characteristics serve both to shape a profile for the selection of future new-church-development leaders and to suggest some ways that seminaries, denominational boards, and key leaders can nurture and strengthen such leadership. The purpose of this addendum is to summarize the practical lessons learned by these extraordinary pastors in order to provide guidance for the development of future new-church-development pastors.

One: Willingness to Risk

The primary behavior of these mission pastors was their willingness to risk. None seemed to lack courage or to suffer from a failure of nerve.[1]

---

1. "A Failure of Nerve: Leadership in the Age of the Quick Fix," by Edwin H. Friedman, was compiled and edited by Edward W. Beal and Margaret M. Treadwell after Friedman's death. This most revealing study of the impact of fear of risk on leadership is important reading for anyone in leadership.

They thrive on facing their fears each day to get the mission developed. These leaders learn from their mistakes and redesign their efforts to ensure success.

> There are certain things you just have to do, and if you are not willing to do it, don't take on the job. You have got to be willing to stick your neck out, put yourself out there on the line for God. (FG 87-02)

> It's about not being afraid to risk. We screwed up a lot, but to me the failure is falling and not getting back up and not learning anything. We've had some expensive learning experiences, but that's all I see them as. (FG 01-02)

Two: Being Vision- and Mission-Driven

Shaping and maintaining a compelling vision is the task these leaders believe they should never give away. These leaders possess a clear sense of purpose,[2] and a large and compelling vision that draws others to join, and those joiners will implement that vision.[3] But they are willing to lose precious new recruits who have a contrary vision in order not to compromise where they are going.

> A clear vision. . . . What we ended up with was focused, and that is why the others have failed: they used a shotgun approach and tried to hit everybody's buttons. (FG 97-00)

> Your vision can be big and exciting, and you have to keep it in front of you at all times. One of the gifts of being in mission development is that we share that vision. I have been in many established churches that don't have any vision to be shared. People don't know how to contribute because they don't know what the vision of the organization is. (FG 94-96)

2. Rick Warren's book *The Purpose-Driven Church* (Grand Rapids: Zondervan, 1995) makes the case for vision at the center of mission (pp. 8off.).

3. I have defined leadership as "the ability to cast a compelling vision, which will recruit others who will largely implement that vision, satisfy the respect of others where respect is necessary, and do it under conditions of stress, because it will mean change and new direction."

Three: Willingness to Let People Go

This compelling mark of effective ministry involves the capacity to be open to growth without being compromised. Many times this means letting go of key people, people who began with the new church, people in whom the vision seemed to be planted. Saying goodbye isn't easy; but for the sake of the future, it is sometimes necessary. This is where risk is made manifest.

> There are people who aren't with the program; they come with a plan, and if it doesn't fit, we have to be able to say good-bye to some of them. It's difficult, particularly for our church, because it doesn't have the name recognition. (FG 90-93)

> People left because we didn't fit what they felt a church was. Again and again as leaders, we had to say, this is our purpose to whoever is out there. So our purpose/mission was key to what separated us from what other churches were doing in that county. (FG 97-00)

Four: Focus on Jesus

These pastors are clear that the focus is on Jesus — his faith, life, death, resurrection, and teachings.[4] Their goal is to make disciples of Jesus; however, they know that to come to faith is a process. To honor the process, these pastors nurture young Christians toward faith in Christ and in a commitment to the mission of God.

> Before I do anything, I need to sense the presence of Jesus Christ there with me. What I'm going to do or say has only a little impact on the kingdom of God. I can't do it without him, trusting that he'll lead me in some way. (FG 01-02)

> I would be willing to do anything it would take to get people who do not know Jesus Christ into a faith relationship with Jesus. (FG 90-93)

4. The theme of "Justification and Mission" at the 1967 World Council of Churches Assembly in Uppsala, Sweden, brought clarity to the centrality and uniqueness of Jesus' proclamation of God's mission.

Five: Mission Is at the Center of Their Lives

God's mission energizes these pastors. They discover that the meaning in their ministries is the impact of faith on new Christians. They understand that the United States is now a great place to take seriously the mandate of "making disciples of all nations."[5] The nations of the world are all here. This challenge is their calling, and they feel accountable to God for its fulfillment.

> One of the things that was important for our church was evangelism, a very high priority. Just recognizing the power of the gospel and seeing people's problems, that the basic problem is really sin and that Christ was the solution to that. . . . There has to be a real deep conviction for evangelism that the pastor and the people must have as well. We cannot be afraid to tell people the good news. (FG 94-96)

Six: Prayer Is at the Center of Their Lives

These pastors are clear about the source of power in their lives. They start the day with prayer and continue in prayer. The constant challenge to overcome is not to rely on what they do but to give in to what God is doing to lead them in the development of this ministry.

> If we, as a pastor or any faithful disciple, do not have some sort of discipline — prayer, meditation life — we'll be empty before we know it. I think that what Jesus was saying is, "I can't give any more until I get fed." Caring for people just saps you. It drains you. That leads back to a fundamental thing. (FG 87-89)

5. The United States receives over 1.5 million new immigrants a year, and there are now few communities that are not multicultural. Most of the denominations in this study have practiced ethnic-specific outreach with new congregations. A new phenomenon in mission is the outreach from Latin America, Asia, and Africa, where mission development uses pastors from such places as Ethiopia, Namibia, Liberia, India, Indonesia (Batak language), Korea, China, and Japan. Many of these churches organize as congregations and become integrated during the second generation. Many existing congregations that were formerly all Euro-American are now reporting more ethnic diversity in their memberships.

If we don't have a prayer life, if we aren't taking daily time with God, then we get so filled with ourselves, there is no room left for the Spirit. It gets to the fundamental question, Who is going to lead this thing? Look at your track record and look at God's. Who do you want to be developing this mission? Who has the power and who has the ability and who doesn't? If I was speaking to first-time developers, I would emphasize that. (FG 01-02)

Seven: Passion for This Work

These leaders have a passion for new-church development. If they were not doing mission development ministry at this location, they would be doing it somewhere else. Their passion is for the building of relationships with God. Their passion is to communicate how much God loves people. They believe that it does make a difference what you believe, and that difference will transform your life.

It's been a thrill and it's been frustrating all at the same time; but I wouldn't trade it for anything. I was born for this. . . . (FG 87-02)

Like I said, it's just wonderful fun. I hope to do it again. I can see myself starting church after church after church. (FG 87-02)

Eight: High Expectations

These leaders have high expectations for the congregation and for the participants in the ministry.[6] They maintain a clear biblical framework and faith standard. They believe that being a Christian means that life is transformed and that this transformation will result in a difference in the way people live.

We say that being a Christian means being a member of the body of Christ. That's the theological part that we teach. We talk about

6. Christian A. Schwartz, *Natural Church Development* (Carol Stream, IL: Church-Smart Resources, 1998), pp. 20-23; pp. 122-123 make the case for high-expectation churches.

partnership, that we do have work here to do given to us by God. We talk about everybody in this place being a ten at something. You have gifts that we need. We talk about everybody in this place wearing an apron, not a bib. Don't come here if you've got a bib on. Put an apron on and you will get spiritually fed. That's what the church is all about. We haven't let up on that one. (FG 87-89)

Our congregation is more postmodern. They want to know the Bible. They want to know what it says. They're hungry. What surprised me about people who are "de-churched" is that they expect you to preach on the Bible, and they expect you to use God's name, and they expect you to do a lot of the things that many churches have completely abandoned. (FG 01-02)

Nine: This Ministry Is a "God Thing"

Pastors of these congregations have a profound faith in God as the real leader/actor in their ministries. They also make it clear that God brought the people to the church because God knows the needs of people and has prepared a community of believers to receive them and help them discover God's plan for their lives.

We have a perspective that God brought these people here. It's not like you're sitting there and God sends them your way. There's that dual kind of relationship where you need to do your work and position yourself in the community, get to know people; but it's the sense that they belong there. I can't tell you the number of times people have come up to me and said, "This is my first time in here." They haven't had much of a church background at all. Then they say, "I know that God wanted me to hear what was in this service today." (FG 87-89)

I've felt like it's part of my responsibility to be very clear as to why this church is growing — that it's not a me thing, that it's a God thing. That is a constant theme around our church. (FG 01-02)

Ten: A Spiritual Relationship with God

There is a passion among these leaders for the spiritual relationship of their people with God. They have a deep concern for those alienated from God and those who never have known God, and they have a passion to share their experience of faith in Jesus. They have a sure knowledge that life will become more full and whole if these people can only know Jesus.

> In our situation, what is important is the integration of the Christian faith: people's relationship with Christ in the day-to-day life. (FG 90-93)

> Whatever our theological underpinnings are or what our denomination teaches in terms of principles and values, we should stay close to our Lord and recognize his presence. That drives me to be authentic for the people around me, to model for them how I make decisions and how I treat people, how I relate to people, what value I give to kids and to older people. I can preach the greatest sermon ever, but if I don't model that, they'll say, "Where does that come from?" (FG 01-02)

Eleven: Humility and Willingness to Learn from Others

These leaders understand that their talents, even their charismatic gifts, came from God. This tempers strong egos with humility. They give God the credit for growth in the church. They also give credit to others. In fact, they delight in the accomplishment of others, because what they are building is greater than themselves.

> . . . being bold, taking risks, but at the same time being patient and paying attention to what's happening in the community and beyond. I think all of those things play into developing a new congregation. I do think that things happen for a reason and that it's important not just to be willing to proclaim the gospel but maybe even more important to be humble enough to say, the gospel is out there and has so much to say to me, and to look for the gospel in the community and the people around you. (FG 87-02)

Having a strong biblical foundation for all that we do. That calls us again and again to humility, to reaching lost people, to being relevant, communicating God's word to people. (FG 01-02)

Twelve: Multiplying Ministry by Giving Ministry Away

One of the key characteristics of these leaders is their passion to give ministry away to others. Equipping the laity to be in mission is their primary goal. This means multiplying ministry through the gifts of God's people. It means that they see their role as affirming the gifts of others and not as gatekeepers. They are team-centered and can build on the ideas and passions of others.

> I needed to create an atmosphere of grace and permission for others to do ministry. People won't catch it — that they need to be in ministry — if you don't give ministry away. The pastor somehow represents a block to ministry unless you give ministry away to the people: letting them know that this is a safe place to come to, that they can risk caring for others and be accepted no matter who they are. (FG 90-93)

Thirteen: Developing Identity

These pastors know they need to establish an identity in order to differentiate their ministry from other offerings in the community. They have to reach out beyond former affiliates. The unique character of the people and the service they offer to meet the needs of the community shapes their identity.

> Our identity was not who we were as a church denominationally; our identity was trying to build a rapport with two-thirds of the area that didn't go to church anywhere. (FG 90-93)

> I know one of the first things we had to do was to establish an identity. Because we were a mission church and we were in the midst of a lot of established congregations, we had to establish an identity with a name. (FG 97-00)

Fourteen: Developing and Respecting Core Values

These leaders also maintained an articulated set of values about what one could expect from their congregations. The people who came to their churches were looking for what would differentiate this place from the general pabulum of "American Christianity." These leaders knew that they had to stand for something. They had to define themselves over and against the popular expression.

> Authenticity builds trust, and that's what we're talking about around this table: we have to build trust with people who aren't believers or people who are de-churched. (FG 90-93)

> I never want someone to come to our church and leave feeling they haven't met a friend. That was a kind of hospitality theme that I just made clear on Sunday morning. Your business wasn't to hang out with the people that you knew the best but to look for those who God may have sent to you that morning. (FG 87-02)

Fifteen: Building and Experiencing Christian Community

Once a group begins to gather, the pastors of these congregations know that the next task is to build a community of believers. The new congregations cannot rely only on their relationship with their pastors; they need to build on relationships with each other in a common mission.

> We build activities that form community, like cells or groups or other kinds of activities. Especially in a multi-ethnic church, we found that people did not gel as readily because they came from very different backgrounds, many from different languages. So just the emphasis of one's unity in Christ had to be held up. So we had to actually put some effort into knitting people together to become powerful. (FG 94-96)

> We have learned that if people don't find some significant community relationships with people very quickly, they are very hard to keep connected to the body of the congregation. (FG 01-02)

Sixteen: Staffing and Team Building

Most of these pastors sought out people who would complement their ministry as soon as possible. They defined ministry as shared and team-centered. They saw laypeople as part of the team even as they added paid staff to their ministries.

> I would have four people at the very beginning: a music person who is creative and can do a children's choir; a youth director; an administrator who is so gifted at computers that he or she can come out with just hot-looking stuff in his or her sleep, plus keep the administration ball rolling; and the pastor doing the outreach and the worship leadership. (FG 87-02)

> I stumbled onto doing something right, that when I look back, was the key for our church, and that was building leaders, building their capacity to lead very early. From the beginning we built a ten-person leadership team in various areas right away. Even when we were small, I was delegating off as much ministry as I could and not taking the role of solo pastor. . . . And God was blessing those things. (FG 94-96)

Seventeen: Building Personal Relationships

The leaders of these highly effective congregations know that they have to get beyond the personal relationships they establish and help people build relationships with each other in order to establish a congregational identity.

> It's all about relationships. You cannot program it and you cannot create it with a set of ABCs and this will happen, but cultivating this mentality within everybody that "You and I have been blessed by God so you and I can be a blessing to the next people." (FG 90-93)

> I was given a concept that helped me back in '87, when I went into training. The concept was that you were to map out a territory and consider every human being in that parish as if they were your member. Your job is to go around and meet them all and figure out

which ones you could let go because they had other relationships and you didn't have to be their pastor. . . . It's so great about how that's the way the Bible keeps working. God is taking the initiative and now we're a part of that. That idea helped me a lot. (FG 94-96)

Eighteen: Going beyond a Personal Relationship with the Pastor

People seeking congregations come looking for community and for meaning in life. They want to identify with others and form a common identity.

> You are the magnet and you do attract, but at the same time you have to know it's not you but God's work that is happening. And your job is not only the magnet there, but you also are trying to help the people understand that they have to go beyond you in order to become the church and grow the ministry, so that people begin to see how they can function together in ministry. (FG 87-89)

> I'm convinced that our new church was formed because of the heightened feeling of loneliness that people have in our culture today and the ways we were able to minister to people who are lonely. (FG 87-02)

Nineteen: Respecting People, Building Lay Ministry, Equipping People for Ministry

The leaders of effective churches respect where people are in their lives; they listen carefully to understand where people are in their life journey. They know that the answer to clergy burnout and to expanded ministry is in the discovery of lay gifts for ministry. They see themselves as members of a team, delivering ministry where the lay members are as important as the clergy in the future of the mission.

> We had phenomenal laypeople who would work hours and hours to accomplish the tasks that were done. But another key for us was to have a very clear vision that we wanted to reach out to the unchurched, that if there is even one unchurched person left in our community, we still have growing to do. (FG 97-00)

I would say in terms of the role of laity that we had broad involvement of laypersons across the board, including worship leadership — a core group of people, a leadership team, that we initially called a "steering committee." And the development of those core leaders with some sense of where we were headed, what we were about, what was critically important, was essential. (FG 94-96)

Twenty: Shared Authority

Authority can be delegated to others, who also get their authority to act from God. These pastors experience the multiplication of ministry when they give ministry away. They have discovered that an important role of the pastor is to equip others for ministry. This maximizes diversity, which in turn expands the potential target audience for mission. This is the intent of the New Testament's "royal priesthood" and Luther's "priesthood of all believers."

One of the dramatic pieces of mission development is that we take this vision and we lay it out before people and we say, "Here is this vision, what do you think?" They go, "Wow, that's really exciting and I have this gift I can bring to it." I know, a number of times, how excited I saw the laity. If it weren't for people feeding into that vision and having a vision of their own that just walked right in, it would have been okay; but it would not have pushed us that next mile that we needed to be pushed. (FG 87-02)

We set a tone and climate that said, "You are the evangelist in this church: you are called to go out and make very simple, come-and-see invitations, the same way Jesus started the whole thing. Just invite them to come and see." Then we have to trust the Holy Spirit to move when they get here. We can't just be passive about that and say, "Well, you know, hopefully you'll like it." We focused a lot on what people were experiencing in their own lives and still do when they show up the first time. (FG 87-89)

Twenty-One: Respecting Diversity

These pastors have a profound respect for diversity, knowing that diversity will add to ministry. This includes diversity of race, gender, lifestyle, and opinion.

> We had never articulated as part of the vision that we would be a multi-ethnic church. But that's how we discovered God was leading us in that direction. To the point where we had someone who was Anglo, and we asked him, "Why did you choose our church?" And he said, "Because of the variety here. I wanted to come to a multi-ethnic church." There were mono-ethnic churches [for him to choose from]: they were mostly Anglo or mostly Black. But he said, "I didn't want to be part of that." (FG 94-96)

> What the laity bring in their own experience of the Christian faith is both good and bad. They have known what it is like in their lives to be a person of faith. They have known what worked and what excluded them. One of the things that some of the members of our congregation bring that is so powerful is diversity of experience. We do have a number of gay and lesbian persons; we also have a number of persons coming from strict Catholic or strict fundamentalist backgrounds. They sure as heck know what they don't want. They will let me know when red flags go up. So they have helped shape a different kind of experience of the church. The other thing they also bring is an understanding of the community. (FG 87-02)

Twenty-Two: Flexibility, Adaptability, and
Style Changes as Congregation Grows

These leaders agree that they have to be flexible. The reality of change and the constantly changing demands on their role, style, and function of leadership require flexibility. Change exists not only because of the organizational change in dynamics due to size, but also due to environmentally changing times.

> The key to longevity in ministry and the key to going through this process is the ability to change your ministry style as the size of the

congregation grows. If you can't do that, the church either will stop growing or you'll be gone. The flexibility of leadership has been reality — I think it's critical. I'm quite confident around here that every one of us has given ministry away. I have changed: I have a certain number of gifts and I continue to redefine myself so that I'm staying in my gift area and looking for staff people to complement that and grow the church in that way. (FG 87-89)

I think that also, among leadership and myself as a pastor, I had to change from an entrepreneur to a different kind of a leader. At the beginning I was doing a lot, pulling trailers, setting up chairs, preaching, and all that. That was at the very beginning. That was during the first few months or first year. As leaders rose up, it's been a great relief, I tell you. A great relief. Oh man, I hated towing that trailer. I realize that I don't have to do everything anymore. (FG 94-96)

Twenty-Three: Knowing Your Community

Leaders of effective new-church starts shape their ministries by the context of their community. They do not see themselves as being in competition with other churches; rather, they know that they have to respond to the unique needs of their intended audience.

I door-knocked on 5,000 homes from July through September, telling families that there is a new church starting, asking what they would like to see in it that would meet their needs. That's where the preschool came from. That's where the adult daycare came from. That's where a worship-friendly worship service came from, by going door to door and talking to people. I also coached a soccer team, got involved in the YMCA, served on the community board, and so got a real feel for the neighborhood. (FG 90-93)

We had to discover early on who our target audience was. It wasn't so much the unchurched people. We kind of laugh every time I say it, but it's lukewarm Lutherans and comatose Catholics. That's who are in our area, the people who grew up in a church but there was no fire or flame lit for them. (FG 87-89)

Twenty-Four: Developing Local Ownership

Top church leaders know that they have to bring the leaders of their congregations along with them. They are not lone rangers. They bring a core group of leaders through a common experience before asking for their support. This cooperative experience begins with the leaders listening to the people, respecting their insight, and trying to develop a response to their needs. It then turns the response over to the people for them to reshape it within the overall vision of the ministry. People have to feel a part of the response and see how their talents can be used to respond to the needs.

> We attracted a very small core from a couple of local churches of our denomination, and when they all got there, they started building what they previously had. But then they said, "Wait a minute, we left that because we didn't like it." They wanted to build a new thing. (FG 97-00)

> I talked to fifty families coming out of a sister church. A number of people said, "We were there ten years and all we did was slide in a pew and slide out. Now we're going to do something about this. We want to lead. We want to give. We want to lead retreats. We're going to bring people into our homes and bring meals. We are going to pay the price to get this done." In about three years, over half of our people were not from those two churches. They were the unchurched, the fringe — they were the dropped-out types. But that key group of leadership people brought in the resources that we needed. (FG 97-00)

Conclusions

These leaders would be effective in almost any setting. They were placed in settings that had potential for growth, but their own gifts and spirit to succeed helped them discover effective ways to grow congregations. In some cases, other leaders who had been placed in those same settings had failed. It is the spirit of this group of leaders and their relationship to the Spirit of God that ultimately made the difference. The gifts of these extraordinary leaders are the characteristic marks of leadership and appear to differentiate them from others.

Additional Challenges
for Women Developers:
Female Pastors Respond

ROBERT S. HOYT

While the female pastors felt that there were some differences between male and female acceptance of roles, most illustrated in their general comments that their experiences mirrored those of their male counterparts. However, they did experience different expectations on the part of some laypeople who tried to force role limits on them. To be effective the women had to resist this limitation and get beyond it as the ministry matured.

> In order for the growth of the church, you have to change. You either have to say, "No, we are not going to accept this," or "No, I have got to relate more to the leaders than I do" to the entire congregation. There are different implications for a woman to do that than for a man to do that. It's okay for a man to make that switch from being the pastor, from being everybody's best friend, from being the caring pastor, to being more the executive type who has to make those hard decisions. I have watched my husband struggle with that. I know there are cases where the developer pastor has to go from that friend thing, and being accessible, to the leader and focused pastor — and it's the level of accessibility that changes. (FG 87-02)

> People expect women to be always accessible. Those are the only roles most people know women in, as being accessible. When we

start saying, "No, I have got to pay attention to this thing," or whatever, we are breaking out of that mold. It's the mother — it's all different kinds of roles — and we don't live in a culture that understands that yet. (FG 87-02)

When we were the ones having to say, "We've got to pay off this mortgage, we've got to do some fiscal responsibility here," that was not what they wanted to hear from the all-giving, all-caring, earth-mother motif, or whatever. I'm real clear to people: "I am nobody's mother, and you wouldn't want me for your mother, because I had a mother who made you straighten up and fly right." That was my kind of mothering, which I think is just fine. You are the one saying you must pay the rent. You are the one who has to say it, and that's a very different mold for a woman to be in, especially a church woman. (FG 87-02)

It gets back to some of those boundary issues: how you move from the developer at all costs, whatever it takes to get the job done, and this five-to-seven-to-ten-year framework is the switching over — call it even the peeling back of our management skin and becoming a transforming pastor. You are the developer as much as you are the pastor. But you also need to scoop your daughter up and say, "Folks, I love you, but I love my little girl and I need to take her home." Then they start to see you as the pastor, and it only comes over time, because she is going to grow up (you get twenty years with the kids) and she is going to be gone, and that has to happen. (FG 87-02)

New-Church Developers and
Their Connection to Middle Judicatories
and National Denominations

ROBERT S. HOYT

Additional lessons learned from the focus groups can impact future new-church planting. These were not necessarily behaviors of the developer but how the system of ministerial selection and nurture might change judicatories and denominations even as new congregations are planted. As a starting point, looking at Wood's trans-ecclesiastical profile of NCD pastors formed in Chapters Two and Three of this volume and the leadership characteristics I have delineated in Addenda A and B will inform the selection process for mission planters. Dudley's chapter helps denominational leaders in looking at congregational development issues from the grass-roots level up, and Guder's chapter is invaluable in reflecting on doing the right things for the right reasons. Together, these components of this study suggest that new-church developers are part of a larger web of relationships. Therefore, picking the best developer will not assure success if the system is not supportive. A support system must help developers maximize the use of their talents in the new development. Likewise, extraordinary developers themselves can add strength and integrity to the larger system.

There is a balance of conflicting behaviors among these pastors with respect to denominations. They are both appreciative and critical of the support structures that exist to aid them. They love the church, but they see its weaknesses. One developer comments:

Our denomination has been supportive of our particular mission. I'm very grateful for that, but I also have had to fight battles. When we were seeking to purchase our land, the executives asked, "Why does it need to happen?" All of a sudden it didn't fit the guidelines, didn't fit the rules, and they didn't know enough. Does everybody have to go through that kind of fight? (FG 87-02)

Another conflict felt by mission developers is a lack of support by sister churches. This is most acute when the church developments are in the early stage:

It would have taken probably nothing more than a letter to the surrounding dozen congregations to say there's a new mission that's being started and it's blessed by the national church, and therefore we would not only like you to welcome them but even perhaps find ways to assist them and help them. So there was very little of that. There was a little bit of negativism, but it didn't derail the process. (FG 94-96)

On the other hand, when they received support from other churches, they did not soon forget it.

I still remember when I was out door-knocking, feeling very lonely some days and somewhat isolated, so I was grateful for the support that I had. This is kind of personal. We had a church from our denomination in the next suburb, not far from where I was; they were our mother church. They gave a special gift to start this congregation. I would preach there occasionally. Their choir would come and sing. So I had that kind of support. (FG 90-93)

Developers are overwhelmingly grateful for one specific area of denominational support: financial support. However, there are unanswerable questions as to how long that support should last. For some, a three-year window was sufficient; others wanted that support to continue longer. This seems to be an issue that must be addressed on a case-by-case basis. Denominations might prepare for a range of years, and then wean churches and pastors slowly as growth occurs.

I'll be really crass: it's about money. I spent a lot of my early time raising money to be able to do things that needed to be done, the resource for mailings and those kinds of things. It's unfortunate, but I mean, you can do a lot on the back of faith and a few people, but funding is very important and it took a lot of my time. (FG 97-00)

In fairness to the national church body, they provided the funding for about two and a half or three years, and there's no way that our church would have ever existed without that, so it's kind of a funny relationship. Obviously, you need their support and you begin your benevolence and repayments and all of that, and they certainly helped us negotiate a loan. (FG 94-96)

I think the denomination is too quick to just let us go, and we end up sort of floundering out there; if there is that support, it's kind of haphazard. Maybe in our church [denomination] there are certain places where there is strong leadership in place that will help make it happen, so that you can get through that five-to-seven-year phase with a feeling like you have some support. But too often after about three years you are sort of cut loose, and that's too soon. I don't think it's fair to ask somebody to go out there and start something new and then not see them through it, and not be there to support them through those critical phases. (FG 87-02)

One further complication in the conflictual balance of pastors and their denominations is that new-church developments and developers are so specialized that often the best help comes from pastors and churches that are in the same situation rather than in the same denomination. The pastors discussed in this chapter serve healthy congregations. Rather than feeling in competition with other congregations of like size and program, their congregations often feel so strong in themselves that they see little need for a larger church structure. This is not an end to corporate theology, but it does indicate some loss of support for the over seventy-year history of the building up of middle judicatories and church-wide functions of denominations. Rather than looking to denominational executives and pastors exclusively, these pastors see resources coming from mentors and colleagues who have direct experience in new-church development.

That coaching piece is really important. In our denomination we have a mission director, and if [he or she is] not really clicking like an excellent coach, you've got to go find someone else to be your coach. I think it would be very important that, if the mission director hasn't had the development experience, then another coach be assigned who has had it. It can't be that they've read books about it or done a doctorate on it. It needs to be that they were really there. (FG 97-00)

We do a very poor job in the church of networking. Other congregations were down the road maybe two or three years ahead of me and I said, "I want to take you out to lunch and pick your brain. I want to know how you're doing it, what's working and what isn't working." It's one of the great resources we have in the church, but we don't network very well at all. But if somebody was starting today, I would say, "Go find two or three people who can mentor you and who have done this and done it successfully." (FG 87-89)

These developers are entrepreneurial leaders in the middle of bureaucratic systems. While their church bodies have the same goals of expanding the church, often these leaders are thinking outside the box and don't want to compromise. They appreciate the resources that the church can bring to the task, but they are impatient with the system and seek to find ways to stretch the church beyond its policies and procedures. Sometimes this leads to "denominational bypass."

I remember something else in the early days: it was a denominational bypass. I did not fly the colors of our denomination. It was meaningless to the people that I wanted to recruit, and in many ways was a detriment, and anytime we did get people who were from my denomination, they came in with an agenda from a church experience that was weaker or broken or bruised in some way, so we almost became the anti-denominational church in our community — and therefore really grew. (FG 90-93)

The church-at-large is experiencing a loss of denominationalism: that some laypeople and clergy have little or no loyalty to a denomination is a new reality. These developers feel a sense of urgency to start new congregations because they fear the present trajectory of congregations around them. They have to follow their vision.

The denomination can keep their hands off; otherwise, you're just replicating the DNA. You're perpetuating survival instincts; you're perpetuating all those things that have made the denomination shrink. I've known where the denomination has literally killed many of our new starts because the denomination didn't know how to keep their hands off. (FG 90-93)

Developers understand that the church is more than a congregation. They delight when the church recognizes their unique individual gifts and skills. They appreciate being asked to share their gifts with the whole church. When they can have one foot in the local congregation and the other in the church-wide system, they feel the greatest potential for fulfillment. However, when the judicatory tries to curtail their mission, they feel betrayed.

Rather than really empowering very creative ministers who might have different visions of what success is about and telling them to go out there and do their thing, both women and men, the [denomination's program] was very much a cookie cutter mold of what a successful church looked like, and it didn't look like churches that were pastored by any of these people around this table right now. (FG 87-02)

What these leaders need is permission to try new approaches for ministry within their congregations for the sake of developing mission. They see themselves as a research-and-development arm of the church. They believe policy can follow the lessons they learn, not precede them. This may require a transformation of the larger church body or middle judicatory from a gatekeeper and problem-solver to that of a partner in God's mission. This is not anti-institutional or anti-authoritarian behavior; rather, it is a desire to reinvent the denomination and its systems. These pastors may be the best resource to help reinvent the middle judicatory in the future because they are willing to risk, they are on the frontlines of change, they are passionate about relating to God and others, and they are intimately involved in evangelizing outside the walls of Christendom.

Annotated Bibliography
Based on Chapter Themes

Introductory Resources: See Stuart Murray, *Church Planting: Laying the Foundations* (London: Paternoster Press, 1998). See also "What We Have Learned and Are Learning About Church Planting" at http://www.newlifeministries-nlm.org/online/aec01_learnings.htm

For Resources on Choosing Location: See Adam Hamilton, *Leading Beyond the Walls: Developing Congregations with a Heart for the Unchurched* (Nashville: Abingdon Press, 2002). See also new-church developments with demographic links, such as http://www.mislinks.org/church/chplant.htm

For Resources That Focus on Specific People: See C. Kirk Hadaway and David A. Roozen, *Protestant Mainstream: Sources of Growth & Opportunities for Change* (Nashville: Abingdon Press, 1994). For a powerpoint emphasis on focus, http://www.namb/cp/powerpoint/cp_process/CPPlongtooverview.PPT

For Resources with a Focus on Families: See J. V. Thomas and J. Timothy Ahlen, *One Church, Many Congregations: The Key Church Strategy* (Nashville: Abingdon, 1999). See more about New Hope United Methodist Church at: http://umns.umc.org/02/may/202.htm

For Resources on Ethnic and Immigrant Congregations: See Steven R. Warner and Judith G. Wittner, *Gatherings in Diaspora: Religious Communities and New Immigration* (Philadelphia: Temple University Press, 1998). See also George Barna, *The Second Coming of the Church* (Nashville: Word Publishing, 1998). See also http://www.ethnicharvest.org/index.htm

For Resources on Multi-Cultural Outreach: See Charles R. Foster, *Embracing Diversity: Leadership in Multicongregational Congregations* (Bethesda, MD: Alban Institute, 1997), and David Hesselgrave, *Planting Churches Cross-Culturally: North America and Beyond* (Grand Rapids: Baker Books, 2000). For more, see http://www.namb.net/lightupthenation/body_ cpt_11_multicultural.asp

For Resources on Vision-Energy: See Rick Warren, *The Purpose-Driven Church* (Grand Rapids: Zondervan Publishing, 1995); see also Rick Warren's website at http://www.pastors.com. See also Dirk J. Hart, *Charting a Course for Your Church* (Grand Rapids: Faith Alive Christian Resources, 1997); and E. Stanley Ott, *Twelve Dynamic Shifts for Transforming Your Congregation* (Grand Rapids: Eerdmans, 2002). For further information on the Episcopal study, see http://www.episcopalchurch.org/congdev/newchurchreport.html

For Resources about High Commitment: See Thom S. Rainer, *High Expectations: The Remarkable Secret of Keeping People in Your Church* (Nashville: Broadman and Holman Publishers, 1999), and Bill Hull, *Building High Commitment in a Low Commitment World* (Grand Rapids: Revell, 1995). For high commitment, see http://www.religioustolerance.org/chr_fut3.htm

For Resources on Aging with Vision: See Thomas R. Hawkins, *The Learning Congregation: A New Vision of Leadership* (Louisville: Westminster/John Knox Press, 1997), and Martin F. Saarnin, *The Life Cycle of a Congregation* (Washington, DC: Alban Institute, 1986). Update at http://www.alban.org/BookDetails.asp?ID=862. For Alban Institute resources for older churches, see http://www.alban.org/researchinfo.asp?ID=1

For Resources for Vision Matching Location: See Paul Wilkes, *Excellent Protestant Congregations: The Guide to Best Places and Practices* (Louisville: Westminster/John Knox, 2001). See also "Graffiti Pastor" at http://www.christianitytoday.com/le/2002/003/18.80.html

For Resources for Building Community Among Members: See Adam Hamilton, *Leading Beyond the Walls: Developing Congregations with a Heart for the Unchurched* (Nashville: Abingdon Press, 2002); and E. Stanley Ott, *Transform Your Church with Ministry Teams* (Grand Rapids: Eerdmans, 2004). Information on one well-known care program may be found at http://www.stephenministries.org/

For Resources for Caring for Neighbors: See Carl S. Dudley, *Community Ministry: New Challenges, Proven Steps to Faith-based Initiatives* (Bethesda, MD: Alban Institute, 2002). See Servant Evangelism: (http://www.kindness.com/).

For Resources That Expect More in Larger Churches: See Beth Ann Gaede, *Size Transitions in Congregations* (Bethesda, MD: Alban Institute, 2001). See church size resources: http://www.congregationalresources.org/ShowCat.asp?CN=84&SCN=109

For Resources That Demand More from Larger Churches: See C. Kirk Hadaway, *Behold I Do a New Thing: Transforming Communities of Faith* (Cleveland: The Pilgrim Press, 2001). For financial contribution by church size, see http://www.pcusa.org/rs/trend9.htm

For Resources on Growth-Energy: See Aubrey Malphurs, *Planting Growing Churches* (Grand Rapids: Baker Books, 1998). See also http://www.alphausa.org/

For Resources That Build on Generational Differences: See Jackson W. Carroll and Wade Clark Roof, *Bridging Divided Worlds: Congregations and Generational Cultures* (San Francisco: Jossey-Bass, 2002), and Sally Morganthaller, *Worship Evangelism: Inviting Unbelievers into the Presence of God* (Grand Rapids: Zondervan Publishing House, 1999). For more on Willow Creek, see http://www.willowcreek.org/

For Resources Suggesting Relevant Innovation: See Robert Webber, *Blended Worship: Achieving Substance and Relevance* (Peabody, MA: Hendrickson Publishers, 1996), and Gary McIntosh, *One Church, Four Generations: Understanding and Reaching All Ages in Your Church* (Grand Rapids: Baker Books, 2002). See also http://www.pastors.com/articles/Gen-XDrawnToWorship.asp

For Resources Using Generational Differences Creatively: See Wade Clark Roof, *The Spiritual Marketplace* (Princeton, NJ: Princeton University Press, 1991), and Gilbert R. Rendle, *The Multigenerational Congregation: Meeting the Leadership Challenge* (Bethesda, MD: Alban, 2000). See also http://www.gospelcom.net/lpea/firstpriority/spring2002/feature_mittelberg.shtml

For Resources for Older Churches Seeking Change: See Lynn Anderson and Leith Anderson, *Navigating the Winds of Change* (Howard Publishing Company, 1994), and Randy Frazee, *The Comeback Congregation: New Life for Troubled Ministry* (Nashville: Abingdon Publishers, 1995).

For Resources to Make Conflict Work for You: See Jim Herrington, Mike Bonem, and James H. Furr, *Leading Congregational Change: A Practical Guide for the Transformational Journey* (San Francisco: Jossey-Bass, 2000), and Gilbert R. Rendle, *Leading Change in the Congregation: Spiritual and Organizational Tools for Leaders* (Bethesda, MD: The Alban Institute, 1998). For conflict resolution, see ttp://www.interfaithresourcecenter.com/conflict.htm

For Resources That Re-imagine Leadership: See Ronald A. Heifetz, *Leadership Without Easy Answers* (Cambridge, MA: The Belknap Press, 1994). See leadership resources: http://www.leadnet.org/ucn/network_ucn.asp

For Resources Nurturing Communal Creativity: See Dorothy Bass, *Practicing Our Faith: A Way of Life for Searching People* (San Francisco: Jossey-Bass, 1997), and William Isaacs, *Dialogue and the Art of Thinking Together* (New York: Doubleday, 1999). See also: http://www.namb.net/cp/Mentoring/CP_process.asp

Contributors

Carl S. Dudley has for the past dozen years served as Professor of Church and Community and senior research staff of the Hartford Institute for Religion Research, Hartford Seminary. He also directed the Center for Church and Community Ministries at McCormick Theological Seminary (Chicago). Among the more than fifteen books he has written or co-written are, most recently, *Effective Small Churches in the Twenty-first Century* (Abingdon, 2003) and *Community Ministries: Proven Steps and New Challenges to Faith-based Initiatives* (Alban, 2002).

Darrell L. Guder is Academic Dean and Professor of Missional and Ecumenical Theology at Princeton Theological Seminary. He has also taught missions and evangelism at Louisville Presbyterian Theological Seminary and Columbia Theological Seminary. His books include *The Continuing Conversion of the Church* (2000) and *Missional Church: A Vision for the Sending of the Church in North America* (1998), both Eerdmans. He serves as secretary-treasurer of the American Society of Missiology.

Robert S. Hoyt has served as Executive for Program and New Congregational Development in the Division of Outreach of the Evangelical Lutheran Church in America. He has also been Director of the Department of Mission Services for the ELCA and has served on the faculties of Lutheran School of Theology at Chicago and Luther Seminary, St. Paul, MN. He has helped more than three hundred congregations study and successfully meet the dynamic changes in their communities.

H. Stanley Wood is the Ford Chair Associate Professor of Congregational Leadership and Evangelism, and Director of Field Education and Integrative Studies, at San Francisco Theological Seminary, San Anselmo, CA. His prior position was Director of the Center for New Church Development at Columbia Theological Seminary, Decatur, GA. His publications include *How to Take the Congregant Survey* (CTS Press). He has also served as chaplain to the NFL's Philadelphia Eagles.